MULTICULTURAL MONOLOGUES FOR YOUNG ACTORS

Craig Slaight and Jack Sharrar, editors

The Young Actors Series

SK

A Smith and Kraus Book

A Smith and Kraus Book
Published by Smith and Kraus, Inc.
One Main Street, Lyme, NH 03768
603.795.4331

Cover and Text Design By Julia Hill
Cover Art *Fish I* by Irene Kelly
Manufactured in the United States of America

First Edition: February 1995
10 9 8 7 6 5 4 3 2 1

Library of Congress Cataloging-in-Publication Data
Multicultural monologues for young actors / Craig Slaight and Jack Sharrar, editors. –1st ed.
        p. cm. -- (The Young actors series)
        ISBN 1-880399-47-4 (alk. paper)

        1. Acting. 2. Monologues. 3. Multiculturalism. [1. Acting. 2. Monologues.] I. Slaight, Craig. II. Sharrar, Jack F., 1949-. III. Series.

PN2080.M86   1994
808.82'45--dc20   94-44188
                          CIP
                          AC

THE MEANING OF SIMPLICITY

I hide behind simple things so you'll find me;
if you don't find me, you'll find the things,
you'll touch what my hand has touched,
our hand-prints will merge.

The August moon glitters in the kitchen
like a tin-plated pot (it gets that way
    because of what I'm saying to you),
it lights up the empty house and
    the house's kneeling silence –
always the silence remains kneeling.

Every word is a doorway
to a meeting, one often cancelled,
and that's when a word is true:
    when it insists on the meeting.

Yannis Ritsos
Greece
Translated by Edmund Keeley

FOR TIMOTHY MASON

TABLE OF CONTENTS

MONOLOGUES FOR YOUNG MEN

PREFACE

One of the greatest joys of acting is playing characters from many walks of life. The heightened life of the actor reflects a need to live life more fully than most people. Like all artists, actors feel passionately about articulating our living experience. Dramatic literature throughout the world is rich in the reflection of human struggle, happiness, and continual questioning. To embrace the art of acting is to constantly enter different worlds.

In this volume you will find a collection of life experiences from throughout the many cultures that people our world. By design we've challenged ourselves to offer a usable collection of monologues for young actors that will serve as exploration tools, while at the same time providing a journey rich in diversity. To be successful in this journey you will have to venture into worlds that are not, perhaps, immediate to your own experiences. To play the role truthfully you will most certainly need to become more familiar with the world of the character, beyond the printed excerpt here. To genuinely understand the complexity of each specific drama and character obstacle, you must dig deeply for both character composition and cultural texture. Happily, as our world becomes a smaller and more accessible place, the resources are more available for your search.

As with our prior collections for young actors, we've selected quality literature by significant writers. Once again we've included speeches from plays, first-person poetry, and cuttings from fiction. Perhaps more than in the earlier books, we felt a compelling need to seek fine dramatic writing that wasn't as familiar – offering a new light on literature that has a very specific and honorable place in our explorations in the theatre. Some selections are from known classics, others are from plays so recently produced (as of this writing) that the scripts are available only through the writer's representative. In all cases, we feel you should embrace the work you set out to do with a full understanding of the complete text. You will find the sources for each play in the back of the collection.

So often monologue collections serve as a helpful tool when approaching an audition. The selections here might be a refreshing and useful choice for auditions. However, since the demands of each audition are frequently different, make sure the selection you choose is appropriate for the requirements of your audition and meets the time limits. We have not considered audition time constraints when selecting the body of this work.

Finally, we urge you, as a young actor, to embrace the rich diversity of our world in considering your own point of view about theater and about life. The theater is an articulate tool, promoting understanding and deep thought. As an instrument in such a vital and exciting venue, be responsible for bringing beautiful characters to life with diligence in your preparation and passion in your delivery. We hope the many faces and souls you create enhance the journey you are about to take.

Craig Slaight, Jack Sharrar
San Francisco
October, 1994

MONOLOGUES
FOR
YOUNG WOMEN

Asa Ga Kimashita

Velina Hasu Houston

Setsuko, 20

Asa Ga Kimashita is the story of the Shimidas, a Japanese family living on the island of Shikoku during the last days of World War II. Here, amidst exploding bombs and the screams of people fleeing for their lives, Setsuko, the younger daughter, pensively eats a handful of locusts that she has taken from a handkerchief; she attempts to share them with the audience.

♦ ♦ ♦ ♦

SETSUKO: A beast wrestles with my soul. It comes at night, hiding in the crash of the midnight tide, arrogant and white, powerful and persistent. Who owns this creature? Who unleashes him here, as he comes to abort our lives and devour our dreams? Yesterday, I climbed in my persimmon orchard to stare at the stars of Obon, the sea in July, and happy children . . . I was one of them. Today, I eat locusts. (*Extends a locust toward the audience and smiles gently as she withdraws the offering.*) The stars move over to make room for the terror. Its eyes flicker fire and bodies go up in smoke. My schoolmate jumps into the river, curling in death, breasts melting into belly into thighs. And I am whole and unmelted. The beast spares me and yet my heart is on fire. (*A beat.*) Mother? Can you hear me? They can take my country, but they cannot take you.

Becoming Memories
Arthur Giron

Hannah, 16-18

Becoming Memories is an intimate tapestry of rural America focusing on five
diverse families from 1911 to the present. Moving back and forth through time,
the play depicts over a century of family evolution. In this speech Hannah
Carolina Vangger, a spirited young Mennonite, applies as a volunteer to care for
refugees from the Russian Revolution.

◆ ◆ ◆ ◆

(*Hannah Carolina Vangger appears in a pool of light. In one hand
she holds her Bible to her breast, in the other she lugs a heavy
suitcase. Hannah wears a black bonnet and other traditional garb.
She sets down her suitcase, curtsies.*)

HANNAH: Please, Tis is te office of te new Mennonite Relief
Organization? Goot. My name ist Hannah Carolina Vangger. I
come from nortern Indiana, outside Topeka, vay outside. My
foder, he has a small farm vay out der. Und he always tell us,
"Seek not dine own goot, but dat of anoder." You vant me to tell
you my qualifications for relief work? I tell.

I finish te eight grade, te time all te girls begins to tink about
veddings. But my foder say, "Hannah must got to high school." It
is a five-mile valk. I tink te girls out der prefer to get married tan to
valk five mile every day. Ven I finish high school my foder he say,
"Now I sell te kitchen stove to pay for Hannah's college
schooling." Und he give me tirty-nine dollar. It took Hannah four
year to pay him back. But I pay him back, ya. So, I am free to go to
Constantinople.

Please, I vish to volunteer to take care of te refugees of te
Russian Revolution. Ya, I know der are no voomen volunteers
permitted. But Turkey is ver te ships are taking te poor Russian
refugee ladies. Te Russian troops have treated tem so badly. Does
ladies are in terror! I can pick te lice from der hair, give tem goot
food, vorm clothes. Some of tees aristocrat ladies don't know how
to survive in te real vorld. I teach tem to sell embroidery. I take
charge of te voomen und te orphans. Chust a vooman can do dat.
Me.

Buba
Hillel Mitelpunkt; translated by Michael Taub

Rachel, 17

A search for happiness, *Buba* dramatizes the story of the title character, a middle-aged Israeli who is in conflict with his brother and himself. In the course of the play Buba meets and falls in love with Rachel, a young wanderer. Here Rachel, whom Buba has just discovered sleeping with his brother, asserts her independence.

♦ ♦ ♦ ♦

RACHEL: It's your brother, he talked about you, not me. (*Silence.*) Said you had a wife and a kid, that they took the kid from you. But I didn't believe a word. (*Silence.*) If you want me to go, I'll go, don't want no favors; I can manage alone, just say you want to be alone and I'm gone. Say it only once and I'm gone. There are other places too, you know. Yesterday I went to a nightclub that has a glass floor with lights underneath pointing to your face. I wanted to practice for tomorrow. I stayed there a few hours, then thought I'd come home to sleep, I thought you'd be worried, only I completely forgot the name of the road. (*Laughing.*) There was this taxi driver outside the club, I thought he must know the way, so I told him a road with orange groves at the end, a stinking steakhouse that closes early, a hill, and over the hill is my friend's house. I said that, so they wouldn't think I was a nobody; you know, with no parents. The driver started to laugh; his friends were laughing, too. I didn't like their looks, so I left. I was already two hours on the road, I was sure that if I kept walking I'd find it, but then it started to rain and my shoes got wet, I was so tired I think I was walking and sleeping. Then I saw this house, it wasn't finished yet. I was sure they'd have a night guard there but even if they did I'd ask him to let me stay for the night. It turns out nobody was there. Under the concrete roof there was a pile of sand – very clean and dry. Then I made myself a bed in the sand; I laughed because suddenly, I was like buried but it was comfortable and warm. You see, in the end I always manage.
[BUBA: If I had a child nobody would take him from me.]

RACHEL: [I said the same thing to your brother too.] I didn't believe a word he said. You know, if he wasn't your brother, I'd have called the police and told them he raped me. My friend did it once to her hairdresser, he was her father's best friend. Because of you I didn't say anything. (*Silence.*) He lied to me, said you left for a week, and things like that. I felt sorry for him because of the accident. He's lucky you're nice to me. You tell him that when you see him.

The Colored Museum
George C. Wolfe

Normal, mid-teens

In *The Colored Museum* George Wolfe shatters racial stereotyping in a series of eleven exhibits that expose the "myths and madness of black/Negro/colored Americans." In "Permutations," the exhibit that follows, Normal Jean Reynolds is about to give birth to a baby she hopes will transform the world.

◆ ◆ ◆

(*Lights up on Normal Jean Reynolds. She is very Southern/country and very young. She wears a simple faded print dress and her hair, slightly mussed, is in plaits. She sits, her dress covering a large oval object.*)

NORMAL: My mama used to say, God made the exceptional, then God made the special and when God got bored, he made me. 'Course she don't say too much of nuthin' no more, not since I lay me this egg.

(*She lifts her dress to uncover a large, white egg laying between her legs.*)

Ya see it all got started when I had me sexual relations with the garbage man. Ooowee, did he smell.

No, not bad. No! He smelled of all the good things folks never shoulda thrown away. His sweat was like cantaloupe juice. His neck was like a ripe-red strawberry. And the water that fell from his eyes was like a deep, dark, juicy-juicy grape. I tell ya, it was like fuckin' a fruit salad, only I didn't spit out the seeds. I kept them here, deep inside. And three days later, my belly commence to swell, real big like.

Well my mama locked me off in some dark room, refusin' to let me see light of day 'cause, "What would the neighbors think." At first I cried a lot, but then I grew used to livin' my days in the dark, and my nights in the dark . . . (*She hums.*) And then it wasn't but a week or so later, my mama off at church, that I got this hurtin' feelin' down here. Worse than anything I'd ever known. And then I started bleedin', real bad. I mean there was blood everywhere. And the pain had me howlin' like a near-dead dog. I tell ya, I was yellin' so loud, I couldn't even hear myself. Noooooooo! Noooooo! Carrying on something like that.

And I guess it was just too much for the body to take, 'cause the next thing I remember . . . is me coming to and there's this big white egg layin' 'tween my legs. First I thought somebody musta put it there as some kind of joke. But then I noticed that all 'round this egg were thin lines of blood that I could trace to back between my legs.

(*Laughing.*) Well, when my mama come home from church she just about died. "Normal Jean, what's that thing 'tween your legs? Normal Jean, you answer me, girl!" It's not a thing, Mama. It's an egg. And I laid it.

She tried separatin' me from it, but I wasn't havin' it. I stayed in that dark room, huggin', holdin' onto it.

And then I heard it. It wasn't anything that coulda been heard 'round the world, or even in the next room. It was kinda like layin' back in the bathtub, ya know, the water just coverin' your ears . . . and if you lay real still and listen real close, you can hear the sound of your heart movin' the water. You ever done that? Well that's what it sounded like. A heart movin' water. And it was happenin' inside here.

Why, I'm the only person I know who ever lay themselves an egg before so that makes me special. You hear that, Mama? I'm special and so's my egg! And special things supposed to be treated like they matter. That's why every night I count to it, so it knows nuthin' never really ends. And I sing it every song I know so that when it comes out, it's full of all kinds of feelings. And I tell it secrets and laugh with it and . . .

(*She suddenly stops and puts her ear to the egg and listens intently.*)

Oh! I don't believe it! I thought I heard . . . yes! (*Excited.*) Can you hear it? Instead of one heart, there's two. Two little hearts just pattering away. Boom-boom-boom. Boom-boom-boom. Talkin' to each other like old friends. Racin' toward the beginnin' of their lives.

(*Listening.*) Oh, no, now there's three . . . four . . . five, six. More hearts than I can count. And they're all alive, beatin' out life inside my egg.

(*We begin to hear the heartbeats, drums, alive inside Normal's egg.*)

Any day now, this egg is gonna crack open and what's gonna come out a be the likes of which nobody has ever seen. My babies! And their skin is gonna turn all kinds of shades in the sun and their hair a be growin' every which-a-way. And It won't matter and they won't care 'cause they know they are so rare and so special 'cause it's not everyday a bunch of babies break outta a white egg and start to live.

And nobody better not try and hurt my babies 'cause if they do, they gonna have to deal with me.

Yes, any day now, this shell's gonna crack and my babies are gonna fly. Fly! Fly!

(*She laughs at the thought, but then stops and says the word as if it's the most natural thing in the world.*)

Fly.

Dancing Feathers
Christel Kleitsch and Paul Stephens

Tafia Shebagabow, 11
In *Dancing Feathers*, Tafia, a young Ojibway girl living on a reserve near
Thunder Bay, Ontario, Canada, struggles to balance the demands of the modern
world with the rich cultural values of her people. In the introductory speech to her
story, Tafia sets her life in context.

♦ ♦ ♦ ♦

TAFIA SHEBAGABOW: Spirit Bay is where I live and I'll bet you've never
been to any place like it in your whole life. The first thing you'd
notice if you came to visit, is that it's small, really small. Only about
forty houses. The second thing you'd probably notice is that
almost everybody here is Indian. That's because Spirit Bay is an
Ojibway reserve. I know how to speak Ojibway too, but mostly I
speak English.

If you saw my house you might think it's kind of run-down
(my father hates repairs and painting and stuff), but inside it's
really cozy. There's only two kids in my family – me and my older
brother Minnow. Minnow's his nickname – he'd kill me if I told
you his real name. (The only hint I'll give is that it starts with an 'R'
and there's a song about a reindeer with his name.) Besides me
and Minnow, there's our father, Baba, and Gok'mis, our
grandmother. And that's everybody. My mother, she died when I
was little.

Oh, I guess I haven't even told you my name yet. Hi, I'm Tafia
– Tafia Shebagabow. (Bet you can't say that five times in a row
really fast!) You probably want to know something about me too.
Well . . . I'm eleven years old and I'm in grade five and my favorite
subject is art. My best friend is Mavis. My Gok'mis calls us Dog and
Bone 'cause Mave is always running around yapping like a little
dog, and I'm Bone, kind of stubborn and quiet. We make a good
combination, most of the time anyway. What else should I tell you
about myself . . . ? I can't think of anything right now, and
besides, you'll find out lots more about me pretty soon.

You might think that life around here is kind of dull, us being way up in northern Ontario, far away from big cities and everything. (Thunder Bay is the closest and it's about a three hour drive away. I've been there five times now.) But we find lots to do. For one thing, everybody knows everybody here, and people visit a lot. And Spirit Bay is right on a big lake – Lake Nipigon. That's where we swim and fish and harvest wild rice. And all around is the bush. Miles and miles and miles of it. That's where we hunt and trap and look for berries and stuff.

Believe it or not, sometimes some pretty exciting things happen to me.

Dream Quest: The Big Save
Amy Jo Cooper

Rose, early teens

The Big Save, set in Spirit Bay, northern Ontario, Canada, tells the story of two Ojibway youths, Rose and Rabbit, whose rivalry turns to friendship and trust. In the first speech Rose recounts a dramatic episode during a challenging game of broom hockey.

◆ ◆ ◆ ◆

ROSE: Maybe I could have played better. They were a good team. It would have been better if Billy had played goal. Most of the time, I got the ball away. I just didn't think about it, and I put my body in the way or else I got it with the broom. But sometimes, none of our team was around, even people who were supposed to be, and I got scared. My arms wouldn't go right, then. Nothing worked: I felt like wood.

At half time Cheemo told me I was doing a good job. He told me just to keep my eye on the ball, not be afraid of it and I would be all right. He said, "Don't be afraid to go out there. Don't stop yourself." I said "okay" but he doesn't understand. Sometimes I am so afraid, I can't move. I don't know why. *Gida-ga-kwonce,* that's what I am. Little baby doe: I was born that way.

I tried to do what Cheemo told me. Sometimes, I forgot I was afraid. The game was almost over. The score was tied and I felt glad. I thought that maybe I could get to the end of the game all right. But there was no one back there helping me. Rabbit should have been playing back, but he kept running up to the front. I started to become afraid again. I told Hack that maybe someone should play back. He told me just to cover the goal and not worry. He wasn't mean when he said it but he must think bad of me. I didn't mean to tell him what to do. I just needed help.

I couldn't see what happened. Everyone was down towards the other goal. Rabbit had run up to get the ball. There was no one back with me. I thought we might get a goal, and I was glad. Then one of their players got the ball from Rabbit. She was big, bigger than Rabbit. He fell into a snowbank, mad. Then she was running towards me. All by herself; that's all I could see. Everything seemed in slow motion. It seemed like forever that she was running, but it was only a few seconds. It was all quiet, too, all of a sudden. I couldn't hear anything. I don't know why. I couldn't move. I tried, but I couldn't get anything to move and then I did, but I fell. Lost my balance I guess. The ice was pretty slippery. She put the ball into the net. We lost, three to two. I guess it was my fault.

♦ ♦ ♦ ♦

Here Rose tells her friend Mavis how she came to be raised by her grandmother.

ROSE: "*Gida-ga-kwonce.*" [but Mavis just looks at me like I'm a bit crazy; she doesn't know Ojibway.]

"Little baby doe," [I explain it to her,] "that's what I am. That's what my grandmother calls me."

[I tell her about the doe, my nisana: animal friend. I tell her the story my grandmother told me, how some people believe what the old ways teach.] When a baby is born, if an animal appears, the baby takes its name, becomes like that animal, and the animal protects it.

My grandmother told me the story many times. She liked the story and she would tell me when we sat after supper, or if we were out and I was afraid. She'd laugh and say "*Gida-ga-kwonce.* You know why I call you that?" I'd say "no" even though I did. I'd say it because I want to hear. She'd tell me about when I was a little baby. "Such an ugly baby," she'd say; oh, she'd never seen such an ugly baby, and scrawny. She felt sorry for me, I was so tiny. She knew she'd take care of me when she first saw me, when my mother brought me. She didn't want any strangers raising me.

Then she'd always tell me, "You can't blame your mother for not raising you. People have to do what they have to do. You can't blame her," and I'd say, "I don't blame her." Then my grandma would get mad and say it was sending her away to school that did it; sending her away to school with all those white kids. When she got out she didn't know who she was; didn't want to live in the bush anymore; but couldn't be a white person, cause she's not. "That's what made her so bad. She's not bad, though; just mixed-up," my grandmother would say.

Last time we heard, my mother was living out west, in Alberta; living with some guy. She sent me a birthday card a couple of years ago. On my birthday, only it was a little late; I still keep it. It says, "To my daughter" and has a poem inside. It was a little dirty when I got it, kind of wrinkled, like someone had crumpled it up. But I put it under a board and put rocks on the board, to smooth it out. Kept it there a couple of days. It's okay, now. I still keep it. One day I'll see her and she'll be proud of me. I'll tell her then I don't blame her.

"Anyways," Grandma said, "She didn't want strangers to have you, so she brought you to me and I decided to keep you." It was winter, "so cold," she said. Grandma told me I was a funny baby: didn't cry out loud. I would just open my mouth, and scream and scream, but no sound would come out. She was a bit worried that I wouldn't live, or something. The first week she'd tell herself not to get too close, baby might die. That's what she'd say.

It was towards evening, getting dark. My grandmother had just got me to sleep and she looked out the window. She was worrying still, worrying about me. Then she saw a doe, a baby doe outside in the snow. It stood there looking at her, didn't run away. She says it told her silently not to be afraid for the baby, not to be afraid for me. It would guard me and it would be me. She said she looked at it for a long time, she didn't know how long. Then she nodded to it, nodded her head that she understood and agreed. The baby doe left, but only after grandmother nodded; it went back to the bush. *Gida-ga-kwonce.*

The Dybbuk
S. Ansky; translated by Henry G. Alsberg and Winifred Katzin

Leah, 18-20

The Dybbuk recounts the tragic love of Channon and Leah. Having been denied Leah's hand in marriage by her father in favor of a wealthier suitor, Channon turns to the magic of Kabala in hopes of winning her love but dies in the mystical attempt. In death, Channon returns as a Dybbuk – or evil spirit, and possesses Leah's body on her wedding day. In the two speeches below, Leah, not yet possessed, shares with her grandmother her beliefs about the spirit world.

◆ ◆ ◆ ◆

LEAH: (*With utter conviction.*) Granny – it isn't evil spirits that surround us, but souls of those who died before their time, and come back again to see all that we do and hear all that we say.

[FRADE: God help you, child, what is the meaning of all this? Souls? What souls? The souls of the pure and good fly up to heaven and stay there at rest in the bright garden of Eden.]

LEAH: No, Granny – they are with us here. (*Her tone changes.*) Grandmother, every one of us is born to a long life of many, many years. If he dies before his years are done, what becomes of the life he has not lived, do you think? What becomes of his joys and sorrows, and all the thoughts he had not time to think, and all the things he hadn't time to do? Where are the children he did not live long enough to bring into the world? Where does all that go to? Where? (*Lost in thought, she continues.*) There was a lad here, Granny . . . his mind was full of wisdom and his soul was set on holy purposes. Long years stretched out before him. Then one day, without warning, his life is destroyed. And strangers bury him in strange earth. (*Desperately.*) What has become of the rest of him? His speech that has been silenced? His prayers that have been cut off? . . . Grandmother – when a candle blows out we light it again and it goes on burning down to the end. So how can a human life which goes out before it has burnt down, remain put out forever? . . . How can it, Granny?

◆ ◆ ◆ ◆

LEAH: No, Granny. No human life goes to waste. If one of us dies before his time, his soul returns to the world to complete its span, to do the things left undone and experience the happiness and griefs he would have known. (*A pause.*) Granny, do you remember you told us how the dead go trooping at midnight into the synagogue? They go to pray the prayers they would have prayed in life, had they not died too soon. (*A pause.*) My mother died in her youth and had no time to live through all that lay in store for her. That is why I go today to the cemetery to ask her to join my father when he leads me under the wedding-canopy. She will be with me there, and after the ceremony we shall dance together. It is the same with all the souls who leave the world before their time. They are here in our midst, unheard and invisible. Only if your desire is strong enough, you can see them, and hear their voices and learn their thoughts . . . I can . . . (*Pointing to the grave.*) The holy grave — I have known it ever since I was a child. And I know the bride and bridegroom buried there. I've seen them often and often, sometimes in dreams and sometimes when I am awake. They are as near to me as my own people . . . (*Deep in meditation.*) They were on the way to their wedding, so young and lovely to see, with a long and beautiful life before them. But murderers set upon them with axes, and in a moment they both lay dead upon the ground. They were laid in one grave, so that they might be together for all time. (*She rises and goes to the grave, followed by Frade, Gittel and Bassia. Stretching out her arms, she says in a loud voice.*) Holy bridegroom and bride, I invite you to my wedding. Be with me under the canopy.

Eulogy For A Small Time Thief
Miguel Piñero

Nicole, 16

In *Eulogy for a Small Time Thief,* Miguel Piñero focuses on a young couple, David and Rosemarie, who are in search of a better life than the street offers. Unfortunately their dreams are corrupted through their involvement with robbery, drugs and prostitution. Tonight, Rosemarie's sister Nicole (who is secretly having an affair with David) brings two school friends home for a proposed sexual encounter with two "clients" David has set up. In the speech below, Nicole tells her sister that she loves David and that she is determined to win him for herself.

♦ ♦ ♦ ♦

NICOLE: Go on and try it, just go on and try it. You think I'm still a little baby. Take a good look at me before you raise your hands to me 'cause you better forget that I'm your sister if you so much lay a hand on me 'cause I'm sure going to forget it and do my best to kick your ass, bitch . . . now get the hell out of my way and let me back inside where I belong. You run, not me, you run, go ahead, run, leave him behind 'cause that's what he was about to do anyway with you. He was going to split on you, that's right, he had all but packed his bags on you, baby, but you didn't know that, big sister, little sister took your man, that's right, little baby innocent snotty-nose sister took your man from you and there's not a single thing you can do about it either, and you can cry and whine all you want but there's not a thing you can do about it 'cause he's my man and I'm not about to let him get into any kind of trouble without me by his side to care for him when he needs me, so get the hell out of my way this minute, hear me, get out of my way, he's mine, you blew it with him, can't you see that you're through, can you see it, are you blind to what's been going on in that house right under your nose, can't you see it? Baby, you blew the game, now it's my turn to play.

♦ ♦ ♦ ♦

Elaine, 16

In this speech, Elaine, who has just discovered one of her "clients" is her own father, attempts to justify her reasons for hustling.

ELAINE: [He's my father, Nicole, now let me handle things here.] Look, Dad, I guess it's time that we stop all this crap going on between you and me . . . First of all, you don't love or like me in the least and I can safely say that I feel the same way about you. I don't dig you at all. Maybe I'm being a little too strong on you, but that's the case. Look, I was planning on leaving you and Mom anyway to make it on my own. I don't need you anymore, and you never needed me, so I guess this takes a responsibility off your shoulders. There has never been anything for me to hold on to in that house, and I know that there never will be . . . and I don't expect . . . if after a while I stopped dreaming about it 'cause you know I always had dreams that someday you and Mom would take a few minutes off from your daily battle to offer me a sign of peace and a favor of love. I had that wonderful dream so many times that it became a rerun, stale photographs of yesterday's family album, showcasing scene in the parlor . . . . life for me has begun on my terms and I am not going to give in an inch, not like you and her, you gave up yards until they became miles of living family nightmares. That's not for me. I lived with it sixteen years and I guess that there is nothing more brutal than that. Perhaps you will disown me. I really don't care, I enjoy being on my own. I've been saving every dime that I hustle to make my exit from that dreary existence that you call living. So drop it already, stop playing the concerned father role. It don't fit you well and it's almost making me want to throw up all over the place, so cut it loose, will ya? . . . You had your drink, now let's go before it gets too hot up here to make it out the door . . .

For Julia

Margareta Garpe; translated by Harry G. Carlson

Julia, 18

In *For Julia*, Margareta Garpe, one of Scandinavia's leading contemporary dramatists, explores the relationship between mothers and daughters and the unique place young people hold in our modern world. Here Julia offers the Prologue to the play.

♦ ♦ ♦ ♦

JULIA: At night I'm an astronaut, walking on the moon. I hold my breath as I put one foot down and raise the other. For a long moment, I hover in the air. The air is dark and weightless. And I'm afraid with every step I take on this strange planet that I'll never set foot on solid ground again. My heart is pounding. I'm an astronaut and I'm walking on the moon. I'm in a hurry. I have just a few minutes to collect enough samples to answer all mankind's questions . . . And I have this great fear that I can never return to earth. It hangs there in the distance, far away, bluish white and shining. Around it, stars are twinkling. It's so terribly fragile. Suddenly I hear the beating of a giant heart. The sound fills the whole universe.

Hey, There — Hello!
Gennadi Mamlin; translated by Miriam Morton

Masha, 14

Hey, There – Hello! is the story of two Russian teenagers, Masha and Valerka, who live next door to one another. First produced in Moscow in 1969, this play mixes fantasy with reality as it explores the struggles and emotions and beliefs and insecurities of its young protagonists. In this speech, young Masha has just climbed a hill and found her friend Valerka, a boy she has met during the summer; it is six o'clock in the evening.

MASHA: (*Offstage.*) Valerka! . . .

[(*Valerka does not respond.*)]

Valerka! . . .

(*Masha appears from left, breathing hard from the climb. She sits on the rock and looks around.*)

What a hill! . . . Lenka told me that you went this way, or I would never have found you . . . How strangely the world is shaped: Where I live, there's not even the lowest hillock – and here, there's a hill on top of a hill. If I were God, I'd allot a mountain for every plain. That would be only fair, and there would be something to rest your eyes on. (*Pause.*) What got into you?No one had left the table yet, but you jumped up and ran off. Where I come from it is considered almost a sin to leave the table before the guests.

[(*Valerka doesn't turn around. He mumbles something.*)]

Oh, Valerka, I, too, have my troubles. Nothing compared to yours, of course. It's really more a disappointment than trouble. It happened two days ago, but I wasn't going to even mention it to you then. My telepathist, it turns out, is a robber. When you threw your uncle out, he moved in with us. You know that small bag he always kept with him – well, he locked it up in the closet of his room, and put the key under his pillow. When he woke up in the morning the bag was gone, and so was the telepathist. Your uncle said he had two thousand rubles in it . . . That's probably a lie – how would he come by two thousand rubles? And my grandmother . . .Well, I'll tell you, I've come to a decision . . . Why don't you listen when I talk to you?

[(*Valerka continues to mumble.*)]

All right, have it your way. I'll tell you the rest another time.

(*Pause.*) Our house looks so tiny from here! . . . And the cemetery . . . (*With careful detail.*) It's a fine cemetery. Serene. And it is so well tended. Just the way it should be, really . . . Oh, Valerka, I never before saw such a beautiful funeral as Gagarin's in Moscow. I saw it on television. With flowers! So many people! And when the sailors fired their salute over his grave, everything inside me trembled with grief – and exaltation . . . And the funeral repast was fine, too. He had well-to-do friends, but they didn't act greedy at the tables. He had as many friends as your father . . . (*She is silent for a moment, glances at Valerka.*) You just stand there. Don't pay attention to a word I'm saying. I'm just talking to make a noise, you know. (*She sighs.*) Ah! The sea! What an element of nature! You look at the sea and feel as though there is nothing else in the world . . .

A Little Something To Easy The Pain
René R. Alomá

Amelia, 18-20
Set against revolutionary turmoil in Santiago de Cuba, *A Little Something to Easy the Pain* explores the conflict between exile and freedom. In the speech below, Amelia, a child of the revolution, is speaking to Carlos Rabel (Paye), a visiting exile. Here Amelia reaffirms her passionate commitment to the principles that charged her people to unite and rebel.

◆ ◆ ◆ ◆

AMELIA: Doña Cacha has been good to me. I was only little when the revolution built the first schoolhouse in my village. It was named Tony Rabel after your uncle. Doña Cacha came up and I was chosen to present her with a bunch of flowers. She said that the future of Cuba was in the hands of us children. She didn't let go of my hand. I was so proud. I wrote to her often. I told her about the monument to her son and how I polished the plaque. When I graduated, I wrote her that I had been offered a scholarship to study in Santiago but that my father didn't have the money to send me. Doña Cacha wrote to my father and told him that she would take me into her home while I studied in Santiago. (*She stands up.*) Doña Cacha has been good to me. The revolution has been very good to me and my family. I work hard and I study hard because I want to reflect the values of the revolution. I know first hand that these values are good and true for our people.

Live And In Color!

Danitra Vance

Flotilda, a Young Woman

Live and In Color! is a one-woman piece in which its author, Danitra Vance, presents a collection of wild and wacky characters who represent the truths of life, however bizarre they may be. Below, Flotilda, a young actress, takes the audience through the role of Juliet, which she is currently playing at Shakespeare in the Slums.

◆ ◆ ◆ ◆

FLOTILDA: I'm Flotilda Williams. I'm a classical actress. Right now I am in a production downtown with a group called Shakespeare in the Slums. We are doing a play by Mister William Shakespeares call *Romeo and Juliet*. And me, I'm Juliet, okay. Now what I want to do for y'all is to extrapolate and explainate on what be going on in the show. The show starts and a lot of things happen but really we just gonna skip all that and get to the good part, where I come in.

I'm at this party, a lot of fancy people there and I'm there with my Mama and the Nurse. Even so I manage to meet this guy. A very good-lookin' guy, makes me laugh with his funny funny jokes, probably got some money. So I like him. His name is Romeo. I have thus extrapolated the title – Romeo and me, Juliet, okay.

Anyway, the party is not even half over when my Mama and the Nurse say, "Juliet, it's time to go." And I say, "Okay, I'll be right with you." So she find Romeo and they say goodbye by touching fingertips like this, (*Gesture.*) completely missing the point.

After that I go home and I'm trying to be asleep but I can't sleep 'cause I'm thinkin' 'bout this guy. How much I want to see him again. How much I want to talk to him again. How much I want to do things with him I've never done before.

Now in the meantime the guy, Romeo, is down in the alleyway lookin' up in my window. Now he not lookin' up in my window because he a freak or nothin' like that, he lookin' up in my window because he like me, okay. Then he start to talk to hisself. Now, he not talkin' to hisself 'cause he crazy or nothin', he talk to hisself 'cause it's a play, okay. People in plays talk to theyselves a lot.

And he say, he say,
"But soft! What light throo yonder windo' break?"
That's when I break through the window.

It's nighttime and I'm on my back porch and I'm in a really bad mood because of this whole situation. And I say my first line, stomp my foot and say,
"Ay, me!
O, Romeo, Romeo! wherefore art thou Romeo?"
Wherefore mean why. She sayin' why why why you gots to be Romeo? Wherefore art thou Romeo!!!

"Deny thy father and refuse thy name;
Or, if thou wilt not, be but sworn my love
And I'll no longer be a Capsulet"
And she thinking
" 'Tis but thy name that is my enemy
Thou art thyself, though not a Montagoo."
What's a Montagoo?

"It is nor hand, nor foot,
Nor arm nor face, nor any other part
Belonging to a man."

You know what she talking about. So she say,
"Romeo, doff thy name,
And for that name which is no part of thee
Take all myself."

Juliet was hip, you dig. She had it going on and she was down. So anyway, you know their families had a kinda Family Feud-type thing going on. Juliet family, maybe like the Crypts and Romeo people could be like the Bloods, you know what I'm saying. And Romeo is not like Michael Jackson, he's a lover and a fighter, okay. Then she see him down in the alleyway and they talk and talk all lovey-dovey lovey-dovey – back and forth back and forth, beat beat, beat beat. They got a passionate blood flow going back and forth. I got really good reviews on this part. Spend some money, get some culture.

Then she say to him,
"My bounty is as boundless as the sea,
My love as deep; the more I give to thee,
The more I have, for both are infinite.
(*Hears noise.*)
I hear some noise within, dear love, adieu."
That mean 'bye.
"Anon, good nurse!"
That mean I'll be right with you, nurse.
"Sweet Montagoo, be true.
Stay but a little, I will come again."

Then she gone. Then she come right back but she has to be really quiet 'cause her Mama n Daddy can't stand his Mama 'n' Daddy n his Mama and Daddy can't stand her Mama n Daddy. So they have to be really really quiet 'cause if they catch them together, they'll kill him n her too. So she say, she say,
"Three words dear Romeo, and goodnight indeed.
If that thy bent of love be honorable,
Thy purpose marriage, send me word tomorrow,
By one that I'll procure to come to thee,
Where and at what time thou wilt perform the rite."
That mean marry me, marry me,
I'm not giving up nothin' till you marry me.
"And all my fortunes at thy foot I'll lay
And follow thee, my lord, throughout the world.
(*Hears noise.*)
I come anon – But if thou mean'st not well
I do beseech thee
(*Noise.*)

By and by, I come –
To cease thy suit and leave me to my grief."
That mean if you not gonna marry me, don't mess with my mind. I can find somebody else.
"A thousand times goodnight."

Then she gone again. This time she gone a little bit longer because she had to talk to her Mama n the Nurse. I don't know why she had to talk to the Nurse 'cause you know she not sick.

She back as soon as she can but she can't see Romeo. But she know he gotta be out there somewhere 'cause they got that passionate blood flow going back and forth back and forth and she can feel him out there beatin' in the night. What she want to do is holler "Yo, Romeo, where you at?" But she can't do that because Juliet is a very dignified girl, and hollerin' off the back porch is a very iginant thing to do. So she say, she say,
"Romeo, hist, Romeo."
Then she see him.
" 'Tis almost morning. I would have thee gone
And yet not further than a wanton's bird
Who lets it hop a little from her hand
Like a poor prisoner in his twisted gyves
And with a silk thread plucks it back again
So loving-jealous of his liberty."
I don't know what that part mean.
Then she say,
"Good night. Good night! Parting is such sweet sorrow
That I shall say goodnight till it be morrow."
(*Exits.*)

My Life Story
Lan Nguyen

A Young Woman

My Life Story is a poem from Naomi Shihab Nye's anthology *This Same Sky, a Collection of Poems from Around the World.* Ms. Nguyen's poem depicts the struggle and pain of growing up in war-torn Vietnam.

What shall I tell about my life?

a life of changes
a life of losing
remembering
eighteen years ago
a little child was born
surrounded by the love of family
so warm and tender
surrounded by mountains and rivers
so free and beautiful

But life was not easy
the dearest father passed away
and left a big scar in the child's head

She grew up with something missing in her
She had seen the people born and dying
    born from the war
    dying from guns and bombs

Sometimes she wished
she could do something
for herself and her people

But what could she do?

Nothing but watch and watch

for she is too small
only a sand in the big desert
no power
nothing at all

She is only herself
an ordinary person
carrying a dream
that seems so far, far, far away

The only thing she can do
is keep hoping
one day her dream will come true

God cannot be mean to her forever.

A Raisin In The Sun
Lorraine Hansberry

Beneatha, 18-20

Set in a Chicago ghetto in the 1950s, *A Raisin in the Sun* is the story of how three generations of the Younger family overcome their conflicts and bring their divergent hopes and dreams into common focus. In the speech that follows, Beneatha, who has just learned that her brother Walter has lost the family's money in a poor investment, speaks to her friend Asagai, a student from Nigeria.

◆ ◆ ◆ ◆

BENEATHA: Me? . . . Me? . . . Me I'm nothing . . . me. When I was very small . . . we used to take our sleds out in the wintertime and the only hills we had were the ice-covered stone steps of some houses down the street. And we used to fill them in with snow and make them smooth and slide down them all day . . . and it was very dangerous you know . . . far too steep . . . and sure enough one day a kid named Rufus came down too fast and hit the sidewalk . . . and we saw his face just split open right there in front of us . . . And I remember standing there looking at his bloody open face thinking that was the end of Rufus. But the ambulance came and they took him to the hospital and they fixed the broken bones and they sewed it all up . . . and the next time I saw Rufus he just had a little line down the middle of his face . . . I never got over that. . . .

[(*Walter sits up, listening on the bed. Throughout this scene it is important that we feel his reaction at all times, that he visibly responds to the words of his sister and Asagai.*)]

[ASAGAI: What?]

BENEATHA: That that was what one person could do for another, fix him up – sew up the problem, make him all right again. That was the most marvelous thing in the world . . . I wanted to do that. I always thought it was the one concrete thing in the world that a human being could do. Fix up the sick, you know – and make them whole again. This was truly being God . . .

Shango Diaspora
Angela Jackson

Girl, early to mid-twenties

Angela Jackson's poetic and theatrical *Shango Diaspora,* subtitled "An African-American Myth of Womanhood and Love (A Ritual drama)," explores a young African-American woman's dream of dangerous and exciting entanglement with Shango, a fire god, and her eventual journey to face him in what becomes a mythic coming-of-age ritual. Jackson interlaces the style of a classic myth with language that is rich, almost bluesy, in its contemporary sound. In the speech below, the Girl approaches and addresses Shango.

♦ ♦ ♦ ♦

(*Setting: Smoke in the distance from a high place. That is Shango's lair/palace. The Girl is journeying. Again, trees walk and stones move. Birds in flight. Bird signal songs. Flight from a big wind, a movement.*)

GIRL: (*Watching the signs of animal flight. Worried. Muses.*) When Fire struts/bewildered beasts scurry. From miles away birds set out a flurry of fear. (*A flurry among the trees. She cringes.*) I smell the skin of smoke. I sense his presence near. His teeth that mark the barks of trees; his eyes peeling a path of leaves leaving the bones of slow bedazzled beasts settled beneath his feet. (*Hesitantly approaches a gate at the foot of a suggested stairwell. The stairwell has steps that are really landings. The steps curve. The steps are in darkness. She listens.*) I hear his breathing. The soft rending of cloth. The soft tearing of the hair of air. (*She looks around her, warily.*) A craziness of atmosphere, near his lair of brilliance and intrigue. (*Measures herself to meet the task.*) My heart wide as a child's. A woman's aroma at my wrists, at my temples, behind my ears. (*Takes out perfume from her carrying basket. Carrying basket is full of goodies.*) This craziness of atmosphere. I want to run. I want to stay. I'm wise enough to fear. Fool enough to linger here.

(*Girl, having decided to face Fire, prepares by dressing up. Adds a shirt of bright colored veils, jewelry. All this from her basket of goodies. A bowl is also in the basket.*)

GIRL: (*Begins tremulously. Gains confidence. It gets good to her. She is downright cocky by the end.*) Most Excellent Lord Shango. You were a god before music/fell and broke/into voices. Before the tribes were marked limb from limb, eye from eye, skin from skin, heart from heart, and brain before desire was formed out of hormone, mucus, and marrow. Before Osiris/you were a god. Before the market of salt, and spices and trade/beads before rice rose out of mud. Before bruteforce/you were a god before the deathhowl/before the Chain/before the Coffle . . .

[THE FAN: (*Bored and jealous.*) My. My. My girl is so extravagant. Sweet child.]

GIRL: (*Loud and determined.*) You were born before Hallelujah, as old as Hosanna! Before the plain and orange-breasted lizard made marriage patterns in the sand./Before the funeral of justice, before mercy, before '27, the flood, when the house was torn from its roots and twins were birthed on the roof./Before the river ran wild before the anger of water/before the beacon, and the lighthouse.

(*Is so excited she rises in her speech. Soldier and The Fan gesture her down. She ignores them.*)

You were a being before the Hawk and the Holy Ghost danced as one on the corner of Celebration and Sanctuary, before the women of the creme sachet and toilet water lay with porcelain gods and works of art./You were there in the time of the North Star/in the Time of Moss that hugs the Tree of Memory. You are as old as the longing for Messiah. Your lifeline equatorial and your heart bleeds back from the long tunnel of the First God.

You have accumulated more pain than I. I have heard of you. I know that I am young. Magician of two thousand smoke screens, griot of light years, people say that I am aglow, a star has set upon me. And I am patient as the moon.

A Shayna Maidel
Barbara Lebow

Rose, 20s

Set in 1946, *A Shayna Maidel* focuses on the recently reunited Weiss family. Although Rose and her father escaped the horrors of Nazi Germany, her mother, who remained in Poland to care for Rose's ailing sister Lusia, perished in a concentration camp. Lusia survived and has now made her way to New York to be reunited with her family. On Lusia's first day in America, Rose welcomes her to her home.

◆ ◆ ◆ ◆

ROSE: (*Beginning offstage; rapidly, running on, as she turns off the radio and shows Lusia around.*) It's not very big, but it's mine, at least, and I can do with it what I want, you see, and it's so much better than when I was living with Papa at the Greenspans' in Brooklyn. I'm sure you've heard of them. It was only supposed to be temporary, but that turned out to be sixteen years and the minute I hit twenty-one I moved out. This is the dinette and the kitchen's in there.

(*Lusia follows and stands at the doorway, looking into the kitchen. Rose goes off into kitchen. Offstage.*)

All the appliances came with the apartment. The newest kind of everything. There's nothing to it anymore – cooking and cleaning and keeping it all nice. You'll get used to it. You know, everything you see here, anything you want, just take it. It's all yours, too. Are you hungry? I mean do you want a sandwich . . .

(*Voice only a wisp.*)

. . . or an apple, maybe? Or something to drink?

(*Lusia turns, looks away from doorway as Rose enters.*)

A glass of milk or some juice or tea? I'll bet you drink tea, don't you, in a glass, like Papa?

(*Lusia nods. Rose offers fruit from the table, Lusia shakes her head.*)

But if you're not hungry, let me show you the rest. Now I was saying about the Greenspans, they're really very nice people, very old-fashioned, like Papa, but different. I know they're cousins or something, but I never could get the story straight.

(*Proudly.*)

That's called a Picture Window Convector in that window . . . you know, a heater. It keeps it warm in the winter. I think they're third or fourth cousins, whatever that means, or she is, anyway, and I'm sure they'll want to meet you, but we can worry about that later.

(*Rose and Lusia are in the bedroom.*)

This is your room.

(*She finally puts down the suitcase for the last time, and waits for a reaction.*

[LUSIA: Is nice.]

ROSE: In here's the closet. And the bathroom. It goes right through to the front hall.

(*She goes off. Lusia catches a glimpse of herself in the mirror, is surprised by her appearance, turns away from it quickly. Rose returns with a stack of towels.*)

Here's some clean towels. This is the big one for a bath or shower and this one's a face towel and here's the washcloth. See, I got them monogrammed . . . Oh, I'm sorry, Lusia. I'm just so excited. I'll slow down, I promise.

(*She does, for a while, trying to be aware of Lusia's possible difficulty in understanding, but gradually she will start rushing nervously again.*)

What I mean to say is I had my initials put on them, all matching. And I just had "R.W." put on so when I get married, all I have to do is add another initial.

Sideshow
Miguel Piñero

Sugar, 15-18

The characters in Miguel Piñero's *Sideshow* are Black and Puerto Rican teenagers – a collection of prostitutes, hustlers, drug dealers, and pimps who present their lives in a series of improvised and real scenes. All have a unique story to share concerning their life on the streets and the danger and pain of existing on their own at such a young age. Here Sugar, who's just been beaten by her "man" Lucky, a pimp, tries to quell her need for a fix and the pain that accompanies her "jones coming down" by resting. She speaks to the memory of her mother, whom she misses.

◆ ◆ ◆ ◆

SUGAR: Mama-Mama-Mama, can you hear me, Mama?
It's me, Mama, it's your baby, Mama.
Papa done hit me again, Mama.
He was drunk, Mama. I know he ain't my Papa, Mama,
but every time you're sleeping he comes into the room,
he comes and sits on my bed and feels on my leg, Mama.
Mama, he scares me when he's like that,
breathing all hard and fast and hot, spit falling on me,
him shaking and groaning like an animal.
I know, Mama . . . the landlord . . . the food . . .
Mama, where are you?
I didn't mean for you to die like you did
but you told me you'd be around
when I needed you.
Mama, where have you been?
Mama, where have you been?
Mama, where have you been?
Mama, I need you.
I love you.
I need you now, Mama. I need you now.
I needed you then.
And you tell me to wait 'til tomorrow,
tomorrow is here, Mama.
It's here and it's now yesterday, Mama.

Mama, where have you been?
Shit, Mama, I'm getting sick.
Mama, me, your baby, I needs me a fix.
Mama, I'm a junkie, Mama,
A HOPE TO DIE DOPE FIEND.
Mama, please, it beginning to hurt.
My legs, Mama, they hurt like hell.
Mama, someone is crushing them to nothing,
into powder, Mama,
into powder, Mama, white powder, Mama,
like the one I needs,
like I needed you, Mama,
like when I laid in the bed crying
from fear of the many papas
that came into my room.

The Surface Of Earth

Reynolds Price

Della, 18-20

Reynolds Price's *The Surface of Earth* is one of two novels tracing the life of the Mayfield family. The complexities of relationships, both within the family and with others who affect their lives, becomes a dramatic patchwork of struggle and survival. *The Surface of Earth* spans the years 1903 to 1944. In the speech below, Della, the lifelong serving girl to Rachel Ravens, tells Robinson Mayfield (Rachel's fiancé) of a troubling dream that lead to Rachel's illness. Della is no stranger to Rob. She is described as Rob's "generous friend who had helped him in need." Although Della and Rob have been physically intimate, Della has promised that she will leave after Rob and Rachel marry.

♦ ♦ ♦ ♦

DELLA: One morning I woke up and was lying down by Rachel, and she started shivering in fast little snatches, hard as pneumonia. I thought she was teasing – she was out on her back – so I leaned over close to study her eyes. They were shut down tight but shivering like her. She was suffering something, so I let her do it. Then finally she slowed down and rested too deep – too much like her corpse – so I woke her up; and she said to me, "Thank you." I told her, "You been somewhere; where was it?" She say, "I been hunting my boy that was drowning." I say, "I saw you. Look like you found him." – "Did," she say, "but I couldn't get him out." I ask her, "Where is he?" So she lie there – it's early; nobody up but us, not even Mr. Raven – and tell me, "Della, I had this boy that was close to me as skin; but I woke up one night, and he won't there with me. I stripped down the bed to see where he hiding, right down to the slats, or maybe in my sleep I had smothered his face. I was having to feel; the whole thing was dark. But I still couldn't find him; so I ran outside in my thin nightgown – it was summer and hot – and went to some woods and called round there till he answered his name, way off, real weak. Then I kept on calling, and he answer his name, and I finally get to him. I still can't see him, but I hear him speak his name, and he's struggling to float. It seem like a pond and him at the edge. I try to reach out; fall down on my stomach and stretch way toward him. And I do get to touch him – brush his fingers: so weak they can't hold me now – but he go on sinking, and I run back home." That was when she could rest again, when I saw her resting.

Talking Bones
Shay Youngblood

Eila, early 20s

Shay Youngblood's mysterious play deals with three generations of women: Ruth, in her early sixties; Baybay, Ruth's daughter, and Baybay's daughter, Eila. Ruth hears voices – voices that she feels are intended to advise her and her family. As Ruth approaches the final days of her life, she becomes more impassioned about the voices and their message. At odds with Ruth is her daughter, Baybay, who seeks escape from the confines of this family and responsibility. In the middle is Eila, who cares equally for Baybay and her grandmother, Ruth. In the first speech below, Eila attempts to gain some understanding from her mother about the voices she has heard.

◆ ◆ ◆ ◆

EILA: Mama, I'm scared. Loud music and voices and colors wake me up in the middle of the night. I went to see a madrina, a rootwoman, a healer, way up in Harlem. She burned blue incense, prayed over me and threw bones on the floor. (*Pause. Eila begins a trance. Sing-song as if the words are unrelated, nonsense. Her level of energy increases as she is taken over by the trance. Lights change.*) I am walking down 42nd Street. Just walking, walking past the bright lights, the greasy smells, the loud colors. Car horns honking, leather-faced junkies trading dope in English, Spanish and Japanese. (*Beat.*) A black Jesus is testifying about dying on the cross. I hear music. A heartbeat, a steady drumming, a chorus of voices that burst into a beautiful convulsion. Sounds; humming, a cat in heat, a woman screaming in the eye of an orgasm. I see them, frame by frame. There are homeless people stacked one on top of the other. People in high-heeled shoes are dancing on top of their bodies, pretending not to hear their moans. I look down at my feet and I am wearing a pair of silver, spike-heeled shoes. I am standing in the middle of a woman's stomach. I look right into her eyes. She is scared just like me. She is screaming but no sound is coming out of her mouth. Things are out of sync. I remember that no one is looking into their eyes so I start yelling over the music and sounds and smells for everybody to "Look into their eyes. Look into their eyes." (*End trance.*) When I came to myself I was standing in the same spot and no time had passed.

✦ ✦ ✦ ✦

Eila, early 20s
In this speech, Eila addresses Oz, a homeless man who's come into the
Ancestor's Books & Breakfast, the residence of Eila, her mother and
grandmother.

EILA: When I was a little girl my mama put in a pinch of love with a short-handled spoon. Grammie's recipe was two cupped hands full of kindness. I add to that James Baldwin's fever, Maya Angelou's fire, Ntozake Shange's politics, Alice Walker's vision and Margaret Walker's never forget. I sprinkle words in the soup, words that bubble up to the top, then break into action. I stir in all the compassion I can find and a few tears and a few less fears. When I taste the soup I see things. I know things. (*Eila tastes the soup then trances.*) I see her seven month belly sleeping on cold concrete at the bottom of the subway stairs with the vibrations of well-fed feet and look-away eyes as her lullaby. Two ears to the ground, four eyes closed, dreaming of someplace safe, someplace warm, someplace wanted. (*End trance.*) It hurts to look away.

♦ ♦ ♦ ♦

Eila, early 20s
In this final speech, Eila, in a trance, recounts to her mother, Baybay, a vision
that came to her.

EILA: He had soup this morning. I fed his soul. (*Trance.*) When I step off the train I feel the suffering. I see hunger and broken people. (*Eila's music.*) They ask me for money. I empty my pockets. I eat in restaurants with white linen on the tables, I see hungry minds in the window. I put leftovers from the Chinese restaurant on top of a garbage can and leave a pair of clean chopsticks and a napkin for the woman wearing a blue blanket tied with rope. She is chewing on bread she peels from cracks in the sidewalk. I take off my shoes and walk up to women and men I don't know and I kiss them on the lips in broad daylight. I kiss a woman with holes in her shoes. I kiss her on the mouth. I kiss a man missing teeth and the third finger of his left hand. A man is lying on the steps of a church. A policeman comes to wake him up and move him on. The man says that he has nowhere to go and wants to go to jail. The policeman tells the man that he can't take him to jail unless he commits a crime. The man says, "What crime do I have to commit to be given some food to eat? I'm cold and tired." The policeman says any crime will do. When the policeman turns his back the man throws a rock and breaks a stained glass window in the church. (*End trance.*) It's not right. Something is wrong with this picture. I don't eat or sleep for three days. On the fourth day I have a vision. That the world is a watermelon and everybody can eat from its juicy pink flesh and drink the sweet juice. The seeds are large, warm cocoons for sleeping.

Troubled Waters
Brian Kral

Bet, 15

In *Troubled Waters,* Brian Kral uses as his jumping off point a series of newspaper articles he read that dealt with hunters converging in a "mercy kill" of deer. Set in an area of the Florida Everglades, the play centers around two brothers, J.D. and Michael, their sister, Sandra, and their friend, Bet, an American-Indian girl. After recent droughts and later flooding weaken the deer population, government officials decide to kill the undernourished deer in order to save healthy deer. When there is a large public outcry against this, the children are forced to consider the moral and ecological issues raised by such a "mercy kill." In the speech that follows, Bet stands alone facing the audience.

◆ ◆ ◆ ◆

BET: The night before the hunt, I woke up from a dream. I was standin' in the water at the Everglades, with saw grass weavin' around me like in a breeze. A whistlin' breeze. (*Slight pause.*) The water was cold, 'cause it was just before mornin'. And it came up to my knees, but it didn't bother me. I was lookin' at a dark shape, standin' across from me on a small hummock of land in the middle of the water. The grassy waters, the Indians called it. And the dark shape was a deer, tall as me at the shoulders. A nine-pointer. Proud. (*Slight pause.*) The sun came up, red as ever. It bounced off the water like strikin' a shield, that's how smooth it was. And it lit up that buck with a shimmerin' light, like it would swallow 'im up. (*Slight pause.*) Then that deer and his island started to sink – to just sink into red waves of heat . . . and as he was sinkin', I felt the water 'round me slowly rise, like I was sinkin' too, but it was cold . . . I watched him and he never moved. His head stayed still and proud the whole while. He didn't disturb the water. (*Slight pause.*) When he'd sunk out of sight, I started to swim. I climbed onto land, and let the sun try to warm me. I wrung out my clothes and laid them on rocks. (*Slight pause. The music fades away.*) And I woke up thinkin', he was supposed to die. (*Slight pause.*) I never remembered a dream like that. (*Pause. Airboats can be heard distantly.*) Sunday at six A.M. the hunt started. And I forgot about dreams for awhile. (*The sound of the airboats grows louder.*) Until I saw J.D. runnin' through the Everglades.

WOMBmanWARs
Judith Alexa Jackson

Anima/Animus, ageless

Judith Alexa Jackson created *WOMBmanWARs* out of her reaction to the Anita Hill-Clarence Thomas hearings. Ms. Jackson puts forth the view that if "we all have some woman in us and we all have some man in us, then the Hill-Thomas event was a form of self-bashing rather than woman-bashing." In *WOMBmanWARs* she demonstrates that there are constant wars that go on within women as they try "to be whole in the world." In the speech that follows, Anima/Animus, fetus/spirit child who represents the male/female that exists in all of us, has just sprung forth from her mother's womb.

♦ ♦ ♦ ♦

ANIMA/ANIMUS: (*To audience.*) That's my mother.

(*She poses as Danny crushing the beer can.*) That's my father. (*Poses as Sapphire wiping hands nervously on dish towel.*) That's my mother. (*Poses as Danny straddling a chair.*) That's my father. (*Now stands masculine.*) That's my mother. (*Now stands feminine.*) That's my father. (*She moves to center stage.*) And I'm the child she thinks she lost.

Why did I mess up? Everything was going just fine. I was all set. Cells were developing well. Had all my fingers and toes. All I had left to do was to file away information into my medulla oblongata. The medulla oblongata. The fate-knot. That knotty ball of muscular tissue between the left and right sides of your soul. Ties together the threads of your life. Keeps track of your history that's still to come.

When my parents tied the knot, they bound their life threads as one and I was created as equal halves of them both. I am my mother. I am my father. I am the map carved from the roads built by their two lives. I am Anima/Animus.

Anima you don't hear so much about these days. Can't even find it in the dictionary. It means female soul, from the roots an, "heavenly," and ma, "mother," recalling a time when all souls emanated from the Heavenly Mother. When all souls were male and female. When all souls were Anima/Animus.

Well, that's how it was long ago. But, somewhere in the

middle of Herstory, history intervened. Where once both sides were considered equal — the woman side became the sequel. Don't soundbites simplify things? I'm using soundbites because attention spans are so short in the twentieth century.

To make a long story commercial length, Anima got pushed off the page when some all-knowing know-it-all declared that souls needed redeeming. A savior came along in the body of a man and all praises be folks started believing he was a savior for men only. So the male half was redeemed and walked around all pumped up. I'm bad. I'm bad. The female half shrunk down like an out-of-date coupon. Unredeemable. Centuries went by as the world awaited the coming of a female savior. And let me tell you now. No one's coming. Save your Self.

I can still remember that stuff because I live here in dreamtime where most of you only sleep. What I can't remember is why souls ever had to be redeemed in the first place. (*Crosses into kitchen and submerges into Sapphire.*) I'm waiting for them to call up another child.

♦ ♦ ♦ ♦

Danisha, 12
In this speech, Danisha, daughter/girl child, is coaxed into a playmate's makeshift tepee.

DANISHA: (*To playmate.*) I can see your ol' tepee from here, Jerome. I don't have to go inside if I don't want to. My mommy said I don't have to do anything I don't want to do and I don't want to so I don't have to my mommy said.

NO! Jerome, read my lips. (*She rolls her eyes with much attitude.*) I. DO. NOT. WANT. TO. GO. INSIDE. YOUR. HOME-MADE. TEPEE!

Anyway your mommy didn't give you permission to use her blankets to make no tepee. Did not. Not. Not. Not Not Not NOT. (*Dances in circle and sings personal chant.*) Go Danisha. Go Danisha. Go Danisha. I know you Jerome since you was a baby. Now you a boy and probably got somethin' in there that's gonna scare me.

What you say? You got cake inside. CAKE!!!? (*She licks her lips.*) What kind of cake? (*She tries to look inside.*) Chocolate marshmallow M&M sprinkles and peanut butter on top? Yeah! I want to see THAT! (*She begins to go in, then changes her mind.*) You go inside and bring it out here so I can see it! (*She laughs and does dance/chant again.*) GO DANISHA. GO. DANISHA. GO DANISHA.

You crying? You not crying. You pretend crying. Why are you crying? I don't want to go inside, Jerome. Stop crying. Jerome, stop crying. (*Pause.*) All right . . . if I go in, I can leave whenever I want to. Right? Ain't nothing in their gonna scare me. Right. It's just a tepee. Right . . . and cake. (*She steps inside warily.*)

MONOLOGUES
FOR
YOUNG MEN

¿De Dónde?

Mary Gallagher

Alirio, teenager

Mary Gallagher's compelling drama depicts the lives of Hispanics in the Rio Grande Valley of Texas and is concerned with the rights of refugees and their encounter with the INS (Immigration and Naturalization Service). The title refers to the shortened Spanish phrase for the question "Where are you from?" This is the first phrase heard by Hispanics suspected of being aliens. In the speech below, Alirio, a Salvadoran refugee and student activist, talks with Kathleen, an Anglo nun, about the conditions in the Processing Center.

◆ ◆ ◆ ◆

ALIRIO: This place is like a zoo.

[KATHLEEN: . . . The Processing Center?]

ALIRIO: We call it the corralón, the big corral for animals. We're penned up here, and anyone can ask us anything they want . . . as children tie an animal and poke it with a stick.

(*Pause.*)

[KATHLEEN: I'm sorry.]

ALIRIO: You say you are a friend. Many come here and say this. They all want to know my story. But I am a prisoner of your government, which buys the arms to keep my people down! Every time I tell my story it's another risk!

[KATHLEEN: I know, but I'm just trying to find out the truth –]

ALIRIO: Go to El Salvador! Go with the poor in the barrios, teach them about their rights. Ask the government to give them back the disappeared. Or just to give them sewers, so their children are not dying because they have to drink the water poisoned with their own shit! Or ask for the schoolbooks the United States sent money for many years ago, for the school that still today has no books, no desks, no pens, no paper . . . speak one word for the poor! And when the dark van comes for you, then you have a right to ask, who are the leaders?

(*Pause.*)

[KATHLEEN: I'm afraid to go to El Salvador.]

ALIRIO: [I also.] (*Long beat.*) But I'm afraid here too. At home, I've seen U.S. officers directing Salvadoran troops – kneeling in the street and firing guns into our people. When the police let me go, I knew I had to leave the country – but when friends told me that I might get asylum in the U.S., I said they were crazy. But your leaders are so crazy that I thought it might be true. I had the Red Cross papers proving that I was tortured, I had the advertisement that my family put in the newspaper when I was disappeared . . . so I came to the United States and I found the shelter run by Sister Lillian. I started school. I had a lawyer who was helping me. And then one day as I came out of school, there was a van, with dark glass windows. And now I am in this prison seven months. The prison of your government, which keeps my people down.

Dream Quest: The Big Save

Amy Jo Cooper

Rabbit, early teens

The Big Save, set in Spirit Bay, northern Ontario, Canada, tells the story of two Ojibway youths, Rose and Rabbit, whose rivalry turns to friendship and trust. In the first speech Rabbit relives a dramatic episode during a challenging game of broom hockey; he has just warned his teammate Rose: "You better not goof up today because I don't want to lose."

♦ ♦ ♦ ♦

RABBIT: When I saw that other team, I thought, "No way we'll lose this one. They have more girls than we do." I was a bit wrong about that; they were tougher than I thought. But that was okay. It just meant that we had to play that much harder.

I played the best; made a couple of really great saves. Mavis kept yelling at me to quit hogging the ball, but I wasn't going to let it get too far out of my sight. Not with Rose in goal. My plan was to keep the ball as far away from her as possible. She managed somehow to make a few saves. Mostly with dumb luck, bad shooting on the other team's part. A couple of times, the ball just bounced right off her because she was in the way. Cheemo yelled, "Great save, Rose." Great save, give me a break. It was just because she's such a lump that she managed to save it. No skill involved there. I guess because he's the coach, he has to encourage her.

I made our first goal. It was excellent. Hack started to pass the ball to Mavis, but I could see she wouldn't be able to do much with it, so I intercepted. Good thing, too, because I pushed past their defense and slammed it right into the net to score. Mavis was a bit ticked off, but a goal's a goal, eh. The glory didn't last too long; they turned right around and scored on us. The ball went past our great goalie and into the net. I slammed my broom down, because I was mad, I guess. Mavis said something about if people played their own positions things like that wouldn't happen, but she's always going on about something.

It was tied when we went into the second half: two to two.

Mavis got lucky and scored one for us just before the whistle blew in the first half. We held them for most of the period. It looked like we were going to go into overtime; not much time left to play. There was a faceoff. The ref dropped the ball. Hack managed to knock it away from their forward, but Rocky couldn't get to it. One of their defense scrambled for it and it looked like he had it, but Mavis checked him good; the ball came flying back to me. I ran with it, straight down the ice. Mavis kept yelling at me to pass it, but no way. I was heading right towards that net. Then all of a sudden, bam. Some girl – I don't know why the ref didn't call a penalty on her – checked me, hard, and I went right into a snowbank. There was no one back to defend the goal and Rose was no help. She just slipped right down on the ice, like she was inviting them to score, making it easier. That was it. Game over, three to two: no win, no playoffs, no trip to Thunder Bay.

I'm so sick of losing.

♦ ♦ ♦ ♦

In the second speech, Rabbit is tired of his teammates' "It doesn't matter, it's just a game" attitude every time they lose a game.

RABBIT: It sure wasn't fun, watching the other team being real happy after the game. They were all giving me a hard time, saying, "Hey, star" and "Want maybe I should teach you how to play broomball?" Stuff like that. Man, where do they get off? I sure would like to see them play the team I was on in Thunder Bay. Then we'd see who could play hockey and who was just talking.

I was getting pretty mad at what they were saying. Like, it wasn't my fault, eh. But they kept picking on me, giving me a hard time. I walked away from them. I tried to tell them they didn't know what they were talking about, but they just laughed more at me. That made me even madder, so I just walked away. Who do they think they are, anyway? Then I saw Rose, standing there. I was a bit sorry for her, for a minute, looking so lost and all. But not for long, because she made me mad, just standing there, not fighting, or sorry or anything: just taking it.

Anyways, I let Rose have it, good. I felt like she deserved some of the blame; like it was her fault. No way I was going to take all the garbage the other team was dumping out. So I says to her, "Way to go, Rose," thinking maybe I'd show her, teach her a lesson, or something. But she just stood there, like a bunny; like she was this big dumb bunny and said, "I fell." Yeah, well give me a break; tell me something obvious next time. I was being real cool, because I didn't want the other team to see I was angry or anything. So I just stood there, keeping everything controlled – like maybe I was going to explode, and maybe I wasn't – and said, real even, "You fell, great." I was going to say more, you know, really let her have it, but that's when Cheemo stepped in. He told me to go help Hack with the equipment, so I did.

Dutchman
Amiri Baraka (LeRoi Jones)

Clay, a young man

Set on a New York subway *Dutchman* is a fiery and ultimately violent racial debate between a young black man (Clay) and a bold, dangerous white woman (Lula). After first trying to seduce Clay and failing, Lula engages in a vicious verbal assault that provokes Clay to a heated response. A series of biting and coarse racial arguments ensue and the play ends with Lula murdering Clay. In the speech below, which comes in the final few moments before his murder, Clay speaks of the violent passion that racial injustice breeds.

◆◆◆◆

CLAY: Charlie Parker? Charlie Parker. All the hip white boys scream for Bird. And Bird saying, "Up your ass, feeble-minded ofay! Up your ass." And they sit there talking about the tortured genius of Charlie Parker. Bird would've played not a note of music if he just walked up to East Sixty-seventh Street and killed the first ten white people he saw. Not a note! And I'm the great would-be poet. Yes. That's right! Poet. Some kind of bastard literature . . . all it needs is a simple knife thrust. Just let me bleed you, you loud whore, and one poem vanished. A whole people of neurotics, struggling to keep from being sane. And the only thing that would cure the neurosis would be your murder. Simple as that. I mean if I murdered you, then other white people would begin to understand me. You understand? No. I guess not. If Bessie Smith had killed some white people she wouldn't have needed that music. She could have talked very straight and plain about the world. No metaphors. No grunts. No wiggles in the dark of her soul. Just straight two and two are four. Money. Power. Luxury. Like that. All of them. Crazy niggers turning their backs on sanity. When all it needs is that simple act. Murder. Just murder! Would make us all sane. (*Suddenly weary.*) Ahhh. Shit. But who needs it? I'd rather be a fool. Insane. Safe with my words, and no deaths, and clean, hard thoughts, urging me to new conquests. My people's madness. Hah! That's a laugh. My people. They don't need me to claim them. They got legs and arms of their own. Personal insanities. Mirrors. They don't need all those words. They don't need any defense. But listen, though, one more thing. And you tell this to your father, who's probably the kind of man who needs to know at once. So he can plan ahead. Tell him not to preach so much rationalism and cold logic to these niggers. Let them alone. Let them sing curses at you in code and see your filth as simple lack of style. Don't make the mistake, through some irresponsible surge of Christian charity, of talking too much about the advantages of Western rationalism, or the great intellectual legacy of the white man, or maybe they'll begin to listen. And then, maybe one day, you'll find they actually do understand exactly what you are talking about, all these fantasy people. All these blues people. And on that day, as sure as shit, when you really believe you can "accept" them into your fold, as half-white trustees late of the subject peoples. With no more blues, except the very old ones, and not a watermelon in sight, the great missionary heart will have triumphed, and all of those ex-coons will be stand-up Western men, with eyes for clean hard useful lives, sober, pious and sane, and they'll murder you. They'll murder you, and have very rational explanations. Very much like your own. They'll cut your throats, and drag you out to the edge of your cities so the flesh can fall away from your bones, in sanitary isolation.

Eddie opun Edmundo
Lynne Alvarez

Eddie, 18

Lynne Alvarez's *Eddie opun Edmundo* concerns the journey of a young Hispanic American who travels to Nautla, Mexico, in search of his family's past and his own future after the death of his mother. Confronted with deep conflicts between the culture in which he was raised (as a Hispanic in New York City) and the culture he faces in Mexico, Eddie seeks his true identity and a place in the world. Along the way he is touched and moved by his Aunt Chelo and her fiance of many years, Nyin, and stirred with love for a young local girl. The first speech below is one of two scenes that take place in a college cafe in America two years after Eddie's experiences in Nautla.

♦ ♦ ♦ ♦

EDDIE: Can you guys hear me okay?
Great.
Uh . . . yeah, well this poem's about
a kid I met. I mean, I don't usually think
about kids, but I always wonder where he is. I hope he's safe.
The poem's called . . . uh . . . "Pipo Gets Well."

In a world so new
that many things had not
yet been named,
Pipo, the smallest,
almost died of delicacy,
every flutter of light
a heartbeat.
Once Pipo awoke delirious
and cried,
"Mama, why am I
so much darker
than the rest?"
"Ah," his mother sighed,
"I did not wash you
in a burra's milk
so you did not lighten

like the others."
And Pipo awoke again
and pointed to things
asking, "What's this,
What's this?" until
the world had a name
for all things
even the smallest
and the darkest.

◆ ◆ ◆ ◆

In the following speech, Eddie, confused about his feelings for Alicia, the local
girl he has fallen in love with, talks through his troubles with Mundo, a silent,
lonely young man with mutant features whom Eddie has befriended.

EDDIE: Mundo – if you're out there. Forget it!
I ain't in the mood for your little games or whatever –
You hear what I'm saying?
You know – you should take a hint.
Aren't you sick to death of being an outsider, a freak show?
See that's what I mean. You understand what I'm saying.
So answer!
(*Mundo steps into the light.*)
Act human.
You know you got a problem, but in my humble opinion you
make it worse.
You act so damn freaky.
You dress like a . . . swami or something.
You don't talk.
You can talk. I heard you.
Me and Alicia heard you talking to your goat.
So what's wrong with people?
(*He laughs.*)
Yeah. Yeah, the hundred thousand dollar question. People.
Here I am giving you advice and I'm poison wherever I go.
Just like my old man. I mean, I got here and I figured "home,"
you know. Everyone looks like me. The mayor, Nyin, maybe you, if
you weren't so screwed up. It don't help. Here, I'm a dumb

gringo. Back home I'm a dumb Mexican.

Man . . .

I mean it's not all like that. My neighborhood's pretty cool. You always hear about all this crime on the street, but I feel pretty safe. You go out four in the morning, the lights are on, people're hanging out. If I'm short of money – Tony – the guy at Mimi's'll always spot me a slice of pizza. New York. – New York – Hey – You'd love New York. Let me tell you, it's got a bad rep, but it's great. Nobody'd even give you a second look. You should see what's walking around the streets of New York! No offense. I could see you there.

But Alicia – what could I do with Alicia in New York? If anyone so much as spit out the word "spic," I'd kill them. I'd be arrested for homicide. "Crazy as a goat in New York City" – that's the saying? Can you imagine your little goat there – traffic zooming around, horns blasting? No way. And Alicia with that face like an open book. Like a . . . Like a sun. Like a saint. I wouldn't even want the fucking putrid air to touch her. So, which is the worst crime against humanity – taking her there? Or staying with her here?

(*Eddie buries his face in his hand. Mundo drops his stick. His bells ring. He pats Eddie's shoulder, perhaps to comfort him.*)

EDDIE: The last thing I need is pity from you!

(*He strikes Mundo's hand away.*)

[MUNDO: Yes.]

[(*He leaves.*)]

EDDIE: Hey. I'm sorry. I'm sorry. You caught me off guard. Hey man, I'm sorry. It's not like that.

◆ ◆ ◆ ◆

In this final speech, again in the college cafe, Eddie shares through poetry his Mexican experience.

EDDIE: This poem is called "Plane Ride Home" for obvious reasons.

Leaving Mexico behind,
letting it sink into the sea
while the great continents come
unmoored as they pass my window
stirring the ocean into flowers of
foam and widening their arms into
peninsulas; I leave forever,
foundering on the tusks of
a thousand green volcanoes;
memories
streaming from me like rain;
the bells of churches
echoing in my throat.
I am scattered
Blown north, south
into mystery like the unglimpsed
Peak of Orizaba mist-hung
in July. Summer guardian
you've betrayed me into carrying you
away with me. Wedge against my rib, are
you sword or are you shield?

A Headstrong Boy
Gu Cheng; translated by Donald Finkel

A Young Man

A Headstrong Boy is a poem from Shihab Nye's anthology *This Same Sky, a Collection of Poems from Around the World*. Mr. Cheng, a young Chinese poet, lives in exile between New Zealand and Germany. His poem speaks not only of the pain of exile but of the passionate hope for beauty and truth in life.

YOUNG MAN: I guess my mother spoiled me –
    I'm a headstrong boy. I want every instant
    to be lovely as crayons.

    I'd like to draw – on chaste white paper –
    a clumsy freedom, eyes that never wept,
    a piece of sky, a feather, a leaf,
    a pale green evening, and an apple.

    I'd like to draw dawn, the smile dew sees,
    the earliest, tenderest love – an imaginary love
    who's never seen a mournful cloud,
    whose eyes the color of sky will gaze at me
    forever, and never turn away.
    I'd like to draw distance, a bright horizon,
    carefree, rippling rivers, hills sheathed in green furze.
    I want the lovers to stand together in silence,
    I want each breathless moment to beget a flower.

    I want to draw a future I've never seen –
    nor ever can – though I'm sure she'll be beautiful.
    I'll draw her an autumn coat the color of candle flame,
    and maple leaves, and all the hearts that ever loved her.
    I'll draw her a wedding, an early morning garden party,
    swathed in candy-wrappers decked with winter scenes.

    I'm a headstrong boy. I want to paint out every sorrow,

to cover the world with colored windows,
let all the eyes accustomed to darkness
be accustomed to light. I want to draw wind,
mountains, each one bigger than the last.
I want to draw the dream of the East,
a fathomless sea, a joyful voice.

Finally, I'd like to draw myself in one corner –
a panda, huddled in a dark Victorian forest,
hunkering in the quietest branches, homeless, lost,
not even a heart left behind me, far away,
only teeming dreams of berries
and great, wide eyes.

This pining's pointless.
I haven't any crayons,
any breathless moments.
All I have are fingers and pain.

I think I'll tear the paper to bits
and let them drift away,
hunting for butterflies.

Hey Little Walter
Carla Debbie Alleyne

Walter, teen

Set in a ghetto, *Hey Little Walter* concerns Walter, who, like so many other young boys in similar circumstances, seems to have no other hope of bettering his life except through selling drugs. Hope is found in the inspiration of Walter's sister, Latoya, who paints a picture at school of her dream – a family that is safe and together. The speech below is the opening scene in the play.

♦ ♦ ♦ ♦

(*SETTING: Ghetto illusion. Walter is standing with his back against a graffiti wall. A dim spotlight is on Walter. He has an excessive amount of gold chains around his neck. The song "Little Walter" is heard.*)

WALTER: (*Stage right.*) Listen, man, yo, can you hear me? Hey! Look, don't. Please, man. What are you doing? Why you selling out? (*Pause.*) Can you hear me? (*Louder.*) Can you hear me? (*Pause.*) Damn! (*To audience.*) Damn! (*Hears song.*) Yo, yo, yo not yet. I gotta put them down on my program. (*Public Enemy song plays.*) Yeah, that's more like it. (*Pause.*) Yeah, I got caught out there. It happens all the time. Nothing new, right? "Black Youth Shot," you know the daily headline. Nothing new, right? Wrong! Wrong, 'cause it's more than just guys like me going down. (*Thinks, pause.*) Damn! See my story needs to be told, and if you think it's just mine that's where you're wrong again. Yeah, it's 1990 and we're still wearing these. (*Points to chains.*) Yup, they come in all shapes, sizes and colors. (*Points to audience.*) And I sold out and didn't even realize it. (*Looks at watch.*) Look, time is running short and I gotta get on with my story. (*Pause.*) Yeah, I messed up, but such is life. (*Fixes cap.*) Look, I didn't want it at first, it just happened.

Hey, There – Hello!

Gennadi Mamlin; translated by Miriam Morton

Valerka, 14

Hey, There – Hello! is the story of two Russian teenagers, Masha and Valerka, who live next door to one another. First produced in Moscow in 1969, this play mixes fantasy with reality as it explores the struggles and emotions and beliefs and insecurities of its young protagonists. In the first speech below, Valerka recounts to his friend Masha what happened during the previous night's entertainment at the Seamen's Club.

◆ ◆ ◆ ◆

VALERKA: In the first part [of the show] there were scenes from Schiller's *The Robbers*. Carl Moore was played by the bos'un from the ship "The First of May." (*He envelopes himself in an imaginary cape.*) "Oh, humanity! False, two-faced, beastly tribe! Your tears are but water! Your hearts – iron!" . . . [and] Listen to this – it [so happens] that my uncle's name is Goliaph Petrovich . . . He always refers to himself as "Uncle Goly." . . . In one act we invited him to come up on the stage. Nikolai asks, "How should I introduce you to the audience?" He says, "As a representative of the audience – Goliaph Petrovich Sinko." The audience laughed. Next to Nikolai he looked like a midget. We have a certain act – we put someone from the audience, who volunteers, into a chest and we saw it in half with the person inside. The whole trick is of course in the saw – but the illusion is complete. The saw buzzes and sawdust and small splinters blow in all directions. The audience holds its breath in astonishment and alarm. My uncle was scared out of his wits. He rolled out of the chest screaming, "Help! Help!" Ran all over the stage desperately looking for an exit and not finding it in his panic. Now he has shut himself up in his room and won't talk to anyone . . . Guido took five curtain calls. Then my friends and neighbors lined up to shake my hand. "Thank you, Valery Aleksandrovich," they said to me, "You did the impossible and unforgettable." As for Guido, it develops that he is not just a Merited National Artist. He began his career way before the Revolution. There were stores at that time where magicians could buy their equipment, but now . . . Now every magician devises his own.

Nowadays you can't fool the public so easily – you can't get by without electronics.

◆ ◆ ◆ ◆

In this speech, Valerka looks to the heavens and muses about the Stars.

VALERKA: (*He's completely sober, and addresses the heavens.*) Listen to me, Stars! There are myriads of you – more of you than there are atoms on all of our earth. And you, Milky Way! You are like a motionless cloud. But *I* know – you are like the sand in an hourglass. You pour from one end of the universe to the other. And every grain of your sand is immortal compared to me, because it is a star. I am only a man . . . Come nearer! Nearer! I want to reach you . . . Thank you, Stars! (*He takes an imaginary star from the sky and puts it in his pocket.*) I thank you! I know that a single star brings life to only one person. (*Hides another star in his pocket – and another – and another.*) Thank you! Thank you! So many people on my earth will be happy because of your priceless gift! They will forever marvel at your kindness as a gift to man . . . Oh, you countless, blindingly beautiful, magnificent Stars! (*He shakes an imaginary tree.*) Oh, how many billions of stars have covered the earth! With magic radiance you have filled this world! (*He covers his face with his hands. The music stops.*)

I Am A Man
OyamO

Swahili, 20s

Set in Memphis, Tennessee, in early 1968, *I Am a Man* depicts the events following a tragic incident in which two African-American garbage workers were crushed to death in the loader of their truck. The play unfolds through Bluesman, a blues singer and blues guitarist, who takes us back to the momentous strike of the Memphis Sanitation Workers that followed the deaths of the two men. In the first speech that follows, Swahili, an enraged young proponent of the "Black Nation," has come with a fellow brother to help protect Jones, one of the leaders of the strike.

◆ ◆ ◆ ◆

SWAHILI: They call me Swahili. This is my podna, Brotha Cinnamon. He's the other half of the bodyguard contingent assigned to protect you by Commander Whisper. I know you heard about P.J. Whisper!

[JONES: Yeah, I believe somebody tole me dey read about him too.]

SWAHILI: [They lied.] P.J. Whisper trying to bring knowledge and discipline to the community. He feels the community have the right to defend theyself against enemies by any means necessary. He don't mean no harm to nobody 'bout nothin', just so long as they don't mean no harm to captured Africans in America. That's his whole philosophy in a nutshell. And he got a social program go 'long wit dat.

[JONES: What bring ya'll here tonight?]

SWAHILI: You represent the only black power move in this city. Everybody else talkin' and walkin' in step to whitey's brass band. You stepped forward and declared yo'self a black man. You a runaway. That's dangerous in Babylon. These crackers fidden ta swoop down on you like a flock of ducks on a fat junebug. You need protection and the Invaders program say protect you at all costs, by any means necessary, even against yo' will if need be. You a asset to the poor, working people. We here to serve and protect you and yo' family from the people who say they're civilized but ack like beasts, even toward one another. We got a squad stationed outside yo' wife home now. And me and Brotha

Cinnamon, we stationed outside yo' doe. That's it, mzee.
(*Saluting.*) Power to the People.

◆ ◆ ◆ ◆

In this speech, Swahili remains defiant when he senses that the leaders of the
strike may be selling out.

SWAHILI: Nigga, is you crazy? You want us to be what? Parade
marshals?
[(*Jones enters. The Bluesman sits in a corner.*)]
[JONES: Since ya'll protectin' me, I –]
SWAHILI: Dig this, we thought we were protectin' the leader. But
lately something else happenin'. The minister's negotiating,
organizing, giving press conferences. That honky from New York
and his number-one field nigga running the union, telling the men
what to do and when, and the men doing what they told. Ain't
paying you no mind. The NAACP and Boy Wilkins gettin' all the
play in the national press along with Martin Luther King. King
shoulda been glad he was leading a army instead of a buncha lay-
down-in-the-street-and-kick-me niggas! And he comin' back to try
again! Why the niggas always got to be the ones being peaceful?
When whitey get mad at other whiteys, or anybody else, he go to
war. Look what he doin' right now in Vietnam! But he pay the
"knee-e-e-e-e-gro-o-o-oes" to let him roll some tanks over them.
The pigs making plans to kill black people right now! The FBI got
prisons set up for the rest of us. With uniforms and everything
ready. And you want us to march the people right down to the
slaughterhouse. Peacefully! No way! No way the Invaders gon' lay
down and die peacefully, you dig? Day after tomorrow we
planning on roast pig! It's time to resist by any means necessary
like Malcom X say.
[JONES: Ya'll want to lead the black race, but when I offer you
responsible leadership, you ton it down.]
SWAHILI: Leading black people to their slaughter is not responsible
leadership! You be the Christian that get eat up in the stadium,
not me!

I'm Not Stupid

David E. Rodriguez

Roger, early teens

In David E. Rodriguez's short play *I'm Not Stupid*, which was a winner in the Young Playwrights Festival and first performed at Playwrights Horizons in New York, Rodriguez looks at a dysfunctional mother and her abusive relationship with her learning disabled son, Roger. The mother, an alcoholic, resents the attention her husband gave to their son and, now that the father has died, her animosity has grown because he left the bulk of his money to Roger. Attempts by the boy's psychologist to intervene fail and the mother succeeds in carrying out her evil plan to kill the boy. In the speech that follows, which opens the play, Roger sits in a chair rocking back and forth.

♦ ♦ ♦ ♦

ROGER: I was watching the Little Rascals on TV, they had a clubhouse . . . and I wanted a big clubhouse like the Little Rascals' . . . I'm not stupid! You need WOOD to build a clubhouse, and there is a lot of wood in the junkyard. I could get wood from the junkyard to make me a little house like the Little Rascals'. I was going to sleep in it, and Pa too. We were going to sleep in the clubhouse like the Little Rascals. I went to the junkyard and got a lot of wood . . . I'm not stupid! You need nails, I had a lot of nails, . . . and you.need a box, you build it like a big box, but it's turned upside down . . . I'm not stupid! I could make a clubhouse, you need a hammer for the nails. Pa had a hammer, he had a big hammer. Like this big. It was in the house . . . and I went into the house to get the big hammer. I asked Ma for Pa's hammer. She started to cry. She told me Pa wasn't coming back. (*Pause. Roger begins to cry.*) I'm not stupid! I know Pa was dead. Sleep killed him. Sleep! . . . I was a bad boy.

Mambo Mouth
John Leguizamo

Angel Garcia, young man
In the opening pages of John Leguizamo's collection of one-man scenes, the author offers that "This book is for all the Latin people who have had a hard time holding on to a dream and just made do." Mr. Leguizamo's characters are often irreverent but always startlingly truthful in portraying the diverse dynamics of Hispanic machismo. Behind the hilarity is a unique voice that is pointed and honest. In the first speech below Angel Garcia, who is handcuffed in jail, calls home.

◆ ◆ ◆ ◆

ANGEL GARCIA: (*Into phone.*) Hello? . . . Yeah, hello. Ah, can I speak to my mom, please? . . . No, man, I don't want to talk to you right now. Could you just put my mom on? . . . Are you deaf? I said I don't want to talk to you! . . . No, man, you're not my father. Just put her on!

Hola, Mamá, cómo esta? . . . Oh God, Mom, I'm so glad to hear your voice, you don't know! . . . It's your little Angel . . . No, I don't want anything. Look, I'm just calling from the hundred-tenth precinct to see how you're doing, that's all! . . . Why you get so suspicious every time I call you?

Mom, are you drinking? (*Pain creeps into his voice.*) Oh – see – Ma, don't – don't do that drinking shit. You told me you weren't going to drink no more . . . Well, then, stop listening to those stupid Julio Iglesias records if they make you cry. . . . All right, Mom, I'm going to be straight up with you. Yeah, I got into a little trouble. I hate to ask you, but can you come and get me at the hundred-tenth precinct? . . . I promise you I'll change. This is the last time, I swear this will never happen again. Now, can you just come down to the hundred-tenth precinct, please?

She called you? What did she say? . . . Don't listen to her, Mom. I did not hit her, Mom. She's a fucking liar, Mom! Don't believe her. . . . Yeah, but did she tell you what she did to me? . . . Okay, Mom, I don't have time. I have a lot of business to take care of. . . . Okay, okay, it'll never happen again, I promise. Now can you just come down and get me?

Mom, no, don't put Grandma on now! Don't put – (*Sighs.*)
. . . Hola, Abuelita, how you doin'? How's your hip? . . . Okay,
could you put my mom back on, please? . . . Abuelita, the devil
had nothing to do with it. . . . I don't really care what the Bible has
to say, just put Mom back on. . . . What do you mean, God has
the last laugh? What kind of thing is that to say to anybody? Get
off the phone!

Mom, don't ever put her on again. Now can you come down
to the hundred-tenth precinct and get me out of here? . . . It's like
five stops on the subway. . . . It's not dangerous, I take the subway
every fucking day! . . . I'm sorry, I'll never curse again, all right?
Just make that asshole come with you!

◆ ◆ ◆ ◆

In the speech below, Pepe, a young man, encounters an Immigration official and
lays bare the ignorance of racial prejudice.

PEPE: Excuse me, ése, I just got this gift certificate in the mail saying
that I was entitled to gifts and prizes and possibly money if I came
to La Guardia Airport? (*Comes downstage.*) Oh sure, the name is
Pepe. Pepe Vásquez. (*Panics.*) Orale, what are you doing? You're
making a big mistake! (*Lights up. Pepe stands center stage,
holding a grille of prison bars in front of his face.*)

I'm not Mexican! I'm Swedish! No, you've never seen me
before. Sure I look familiar – all Swedish people look alike.
(*Gibberish in Swedish accent.*) Uta Häagen, Häagen Däazen,
Frusen Glädjé, Nina Häagen. . . .

Okay. Did I say Swedish? I meant Irish – Yeah, black Irish!
(*Singsongy Irish accent.*) Toy ti-toy ti-toy. Oh, Lucky Charms,
they're magically delicious! Pink hearts, green clovers, yellow
moons. What time is it? Oh, Jesus, Joseph, and Mary! It's cabbage
and corned beef time – let me go!

Okay. (*Confessional.*) You got me. I'm not Swedish and I'm
not Irish. You probably guessed it already – I'm Israeli! Mazel tov,
bubeleh (*Jackie Mason schtick.*). Come on, kineahora, open up the
door, I'll walk out, you'll lock the door, you won't miss me, I'll

send you a postcard . . .

Orale, gabacho pendejo. I'm American, man. I was born right here in Flushing. Well, sure I sound Mexican. I was raised by a Mexican nanny. Doesn't everybody have a Maria Consuelo?

As a matter of fact, I got proof right here that I'm American. I got two tickets to the Mets game. Yeah, Gooden's pitching. Come on, I'm late.

Orale, ése. Is it money? It's always money. (*Conspiratorially.*) Well, I got a lot of money. I just don't have it on me. But I know where to get it.

Orale, ése. Tell me, where did your people come from? Santo Domingo? Orale, we're related! We're cousins! Tell me, what's your last name? Rivera? Rivera! That's my mother's maiden name! What a coinky dinky. Hermano, cousin, brother, primo, por favor dejeme ir que somos de la mismita sangre. Los latinos debemos ser unidos y jamás seremos vencidos.

Oh, you don't understand, huh? You're a coconut. (*Angry.*) Brown on the outside, but white on the inside. Why don't you do something for your people for a change and let me out of here?

Okay, I'm sorry, cuz. (*Apologetic.*) Come here. Mira, mijito, I got all my family here. I got my wife and daughter. And my daughter, she's in the hospital. She's a preemie with double pneumonia and asthma. And if you deport me, who's gonna take care of my little chucawala?

Come on, ése. It's not like I'm stealing or living off of you good people's taxes. I'm doing the shit jobs that Americans don't want. (*Anger builds again.*) Tell me, who the hell wants to work for two twenty-five an hour picking toxic pesticide-coated grapes? I'll give you a tip: Don't eat them.

Orale, you Americans act like you own this place, but we were here first. That's right, the Spaniards were here first. Ponce de León, Cortés, Vásquez, Cabeza de Vaca. If it's not true, then how come your country has all our names? Florida, California, Nevada, Arizona, Las Vegas, Los Angeles, San Bernardino, San Antonio, Santa Fe, Nueva York!

Tell you what I'm going to do. I'll let you stay if you let me go.

What are you so afraid of? I'm not a threat. I'm just here for the same reason that all your people came here for – in search of a better life, that's all.

(*Leans away from grille, then comes back outraged.*) Okay, go ahead and send me back. But who's going to clean for you? Because if we all stopped cleaning and said, "adiós," we'd still be the same people, but you'd be dirty! Who's going to pick your chef salads? And who's going to make your guacamole? You need us more than we need you. 'Cause we're here revitalizing the American labor force!

Go ahead and try to keep us back. Because we're going to multiply and multiply (*Thrusts hips.*) so uncontrollably till we push you so far up, you'll be living in Canada! Oh, scary monsters, huh? You might have to learn a second language. Oh, the horror!

But don't worry, we won't deport you. We'll just let you clean our toilets. Yeah, we don't even hold grudges – we'll let you use rubber gloves.

Orale, I'm gonna miss you white people.

No Place To Be Somebody
Charles Gordone

Johnny, 19-22

No Place to Be Somebody, which was awarded a Pulitzer Prize in 1969 (the first to be awarded to an African-American playwright), is a dynamic and compelling study of an ambitious black man named Johnny who owns a bar in a black neighborhood controlled by white thugs. When Johnny begins to buy property and attempts to get into the rackets himself, the local Mafia rough him up. Soon Johnny's life – including the lives of his closest friend and girlfriend – is irretrievably enmeshed in the machinations of the underworld, which leads to a violent conclusion. In the first speech below, Johnny threatens his old mentor, Sweets, who has recently been released from prison and seems to have had a change of heart.

◆ ◆ ◆

(Johnny reaches under the bar and comes up with a revolver. Levels it at Sweets.)

JOHNNY: See this, Sweets? My firs' an' only pistol. You gave it to me long time ago when I was a lookout for you when you was pullin' them owl jobs in Queens. I worshiped the groun' you walked on. I thought the sun rose an' set in yo' ass. You showed me how to make thirteen straight passes without givin' up the dice. Stood behin' me an' nudged me when to play my ace. Hipped me how to make a gapers cut. How to handle myself in a pill joint. Taught me to trust no woman over six or under sixty. Turned me on to the best horse players an' number runners. Showed me how to keep my ass-pocket full'a coins without goin' to jail. Said the wors' crime I ever committed was comin' out'a my mama screamin' black. Tole me all about white folks an' what to expect from the best of 'em. You said as long as there was a single white man on this earth, the black man only had one free choice. That was the way he died. When you went to jail for shootin' Cholly you said, "Sonny Boy, git us a plan." Well, I got us a plan. Now, you come back here nutty an' half dead, dancin' all over me about me goin' through a change'a life. An' how you want me to help you git ready to meet yo' Lawd. Well, git ready, mother fucker. Tha's exactly what I'm gon' do. Help you to meet him. *(Johnny pulls back the hammer of the gun.)*

Gabe, 19-22
In the second speech, Gabe, Johnny's friend and the play's storyteller, makes a confession.

GABE: When I'm by myself like this, for days, weeks, even months at a time, it sort'a gets to me! I mean deep down inside things begin to happen. Lemme confess, sometimes I git to feelin' – like I get so vicious, I wanna go out an' commit mass murder. But don't misunderstand me. Because I call myself a black playwright, don't git the impression I'm hung up on crap like persecution an' hatred. 'Cause I ain't! I'm gonna leave that violence jazz to them cats who are better at it than me. I ain't been out of the house in over two months. Not because I been that busy, I just been too damned scared. I been imaginin' all kind'a things happenin' out there. An' they're waitin' just for me. All manner of treachery an' harm. But don't think because of it my play is about Negro self-pity. Or even that ol' "You-owe-me-whitey party line." 'Cause it ain't. In spite of what I learned in college, it did not give me that introduction to success, equality an' wealth, that to my parents were the most logical alternatives to heaven. Anyway, like I say, I'm gonna leave that social protest jive to them cats who are better equipped than me.

◆ ◆ ◆ ◆

Gabe, 19-22
In the second speech, Gabe recalls his boyhood girlfriend, Maxine.

[DEE: Talking to you is like eatin' cotton candy.]
GABE: Maxine was the little girl who sat across from me.
[DEE: In grade school?]
GABE: I stole a quarter from her. It was in her inkwell. Teacher lined us up. Searched us. The quarter rolled out of the pocket of my hightop boots. I kin still hear them kids yellin' "Our theeefer!"
[DEE: Pretty humiliatin', huh?]
GABE: We sang duets together in the high school choir. Neck an' rub stomachs in dark alleys an' doorways. They kicked her out'a

school when she got pregnant. Sent her away. They was sure I did it. Her mama was wild an' crazy. Turned tricks for a cat who owned a Cadillac. Didn't want me messin' aroun' with Maxine. Said I was a dirty Nigger an' jus' wanted Maxine's ass. When Maxine didn't make her period, her mama got drunk an' come lookin' for me with a razor. I hid out for a couple days. Heard later she slashed all the upholsterin' in her pimp's Cadillac. Ha! She was smart, Maxine was. An' Jewish too. Taught me social consciousness. Said I was a good lover. Said white boys got their virility in how much money they made an' the kind'a car they drove. Said I related better 'cause I was black an' had nothin' to offer but myself. So I quit my job. Used to hide in the closet when her folks came in from Connecticut. Listened to 'em degradin' her for livin' with an' supportin' a Nigger. Maxine got herself an Afro hairdo an' joined the Black Nationalists when I couldn't afford to get her hair straightened at Rose Meta's! Didn't really wanna marry me. Jus' wanted my baby so she could go on welfare. She is out there somewhere. Maxine is. She's out there, waitin' on me to come back to her. Maxine is.

Once Upon A Dream
Miguel González-Pando

Machito, 20

Set in New York City, *Once Upon a Dream* explores the world of Hispanic exiles and refugees struggling to build a life in the urban world far removed from their Caribbean origins. We encounter a widowed mother, Dolores Jiménez, and her family, each of whom is tossed and torn between his or her native culture and the obstacles they confront in the city. Throughout, fantasy and nostalgia confront the cold realities of the present and force the characters to rediscover who they are. In the speech that follows, Machito, the blind son, lashes back at his mother, who has accused him of taking a check from her checkbook.

♦ ♦ ♦ ♦

MACHITO: Damn you! (*With his back to his mother.*) It's just that you . . . you don't understand. You'll never be able to understand. You know nothing about the power of dreams. I only wish you could, for one single night or one single hour . . . if only for an instant, you could feel that revealing . . . that supernatural force . . . that takes over all my senses and gives me back my sight. (*Very calmly.*) Ay . . . and this was such a clear dream – I'd never had a dream that was so revealing. I could see everything clearly . . . the slightest details of the train that carries me to the racetrack – the number fifteen train, painted bright red like the sound of a trumpet . . . the other passengers – I could still describe their smiling faces as they encouraged me . . . and then the tunnel, cool like marble. In the distance I could see the station lights – the same racetrack station, only now it looks different than Tony had always described it . . . (*Almost in a trance.*) The lights keep coming closer, more and more slowly, until the train stops at last . . . (*Pause.*) The doors open and suddenly I can see him clearly – no, it's not a vision, it's him! It's him! My own father is there to meet me . . . And I can see him writing the number fifteen on the wall in front of me, and then he disappears up the stairway that leads to the racetrack. As I don't want to trust my own sight, I go to the wall, close my eyes, and feel what my father has just written. (*His hands follow the action that he is describing.*) The number one is unmistakable, straight as an arrow aiming at the sky . . . and then my fingers slowly trace the curves of the number five. Yes, it is fifteen! The number fifteen again, and now I can no longer doubt.

[DOLORES: My God . . .]

MACHITO: (*Tenderly.*) It was . . . it was a loan, mama. I only borrowed it. The day after tomorrow, when I win the bet, I'll give it back to you, down to the last penny . . . don't worry . . . Can't you see, Papa had come back, and now he was taking care of everything? He has come back with a gift – the number that'll bring me the lucky break I been waiting for – I always knew he would return and take care of everything . . . Now you see, he came back, and he was giving me this chance. No one ever gave me a gift like that, Mama . . . No one ever gave me nothing! How could I blow this chance when it was my own father who was giving it to me?

[DOLORES: Machito, how could you do this to me . . . ?]

MACHITO: (*In an effort to make his mother understand.*) Don't worry. I'm telling you: Papa came back to take care of everything. He hadn't forgotten me, can't you see? On the fifteenth of the month . . . Lolita's fifteenth birthday . . . the number fifteen on the train . . . and the fifteen thousand dollars . . . The number fifteen four times – I can't think why I didn't see there was too much coincidence . . . But, of course, it wasn't a real coincidence, and he came back so I knew it was no coincidence.

Peer Gynt
Henrik Ibsen; translated by Gerry Bamman and Irene Berman

Peer, 20

Henrik Ibsen's *Peer Gynt* spans the life of its title character, Peer, a kind of Norwegian folk hero whose mischievous and roguish ways lead him through a fanciful yet wasteful life. In old age, however, he learns the virtue of living simply and honestly when he is reunited with his first true love, Solveig, who has remained faithful to him throughout the years. In the speech that follows, the young Peer has just returned from deer hunting in the mountains. His mother has been scolding him for leaving her at harvest time, and then returning empty handed having torn his coat and lost his gun. Peer spins a fantastical yarn about his encounter with a magnificent buck.

◆ ◆ ◆ ◆

PEER GYNT: The wind was swirling, blowing bitterly –
    Hidden behind a grove of trees, he struck
    His hoof against the snowy ground – once, twice –
    Looking for lichen –
[AASE: (*As before.*) Yes, of course, what luck!]
PEER GYNT: I held my breath, and stood stock still.
    I heard his hoof squeak against the ice,
    And I could see his antlers branching high
    Above my head – seeming to scratch the sky.
    I fell upon my stomach, inched uphill,
    Hidden among the rocks; so shiny,
    So fat a buck – Mother, it was a thrill
    To see him! Even I felt tiny1
[AASE: Oh, goodness me!]
PEER GYNT: Bang! At the sound
    Of my gun, the buck falls to the ground.
    And in the quarter-second that he's down
    I leap across his heaving back,
    I grab his ear and hold on for dear life,
    I'm poised and just about to plunge my knife
    Into his neck below his antlered crown
    When hey! The monster screams, and crack!
    He scrambles to all fours, and in a flash

I'm flying backwards as he spins
And leaps. My knife and sheath go flying and crash
Against the ice; and then he pins
Me – helpless, terrified– by the thigh
Against his flank – with horns like giant tongs
He squeezes me, then bolts toward clear, blue sky
And Gjendin ridge, as if that will right the wrongs
I've done him.
[AASE: (*Despite herself.*) Good Lord –]
PEER GYNT: Did you ever see
The Gjendin ridge? Its length? Its height?
It's more than three miles long, and right
Atop the crest, sharper than a razor's edge,
You're looking down past glaciers, past the scree,
Past many a barren, icy mountain ledge,
And on both sides simultaneously
You see the sleepy water billow
Black, heavy, maybe two or three
Miles down – a distant, deadly pillow.
Along that ridge, he and I
Blazed like a comet through the sky.
I've ridden many mounts, but never one
Like this. It seemed to me the course
He ran would lead us straight into the sun.
But halfway down, a dizzy force
Beckoned – brown backs of eagles floated
Languorously, almost invitingly,
As we sped overhead unnoted.
Farther down I could see ice floes cracking, see
The shoreline trembling – not a sound was heard.
Like dancers, the spirits of the waves
Were luring us to watery graves
With kicks and twirls, not uttering a sound.
[AASE: (*Dizzy.*) Oh, God help me!]
PEER GYNT: Then, Mother dear,
Above a cliff hopelessly sheer
A grouse to which we gave a scare

Trembled and fluttered, then it flapped and beat
Its wings between the buck's front feet,
And – shrieking – soared into the air.
The buck shied back, turned halfway round,
Bounded high, high above the ground
And off the edge to certain suicide.
Above – the black walls of the mountainside;
Beneath – is nothing but the atmosphere.
We cut through fog – it's quiet, peaceful –
And then we pass a gliding seagull
Who flaps off with a frenzied cry,
Causing his mates to screech and fly
Away. Down, down goes the strange procession,
But far below is a faint impression
Of something white – the belly of a deer!
Our own reflection – the buck and me! –
Careening through the quiet sea
At the same wild speed that we come down –
Rushing to greet us at the ocean's crust
To tell us we will surely drown!

[AASE: (*Gasping for air.*) God! Then what happened? Tell me! Peer!]

PEER GYNT: [I'm just
About to!] Buck from air and buck from sea
Butted their heads simultaneously.
Spume and foam flew around us – one wave crashing
Against another – we were splashing, thrashing!
Minutes, or hours later – maybe more,
I don't know now – we reached the northern shore.
The buck did all the swimming – I held on.
Then I came home.

The Playboy Of The Western World
John Millington Synge

Christy, 20

In *The Playboy of the Western World* Christy Mahan, a shy Irish lad who is hired on to clean pots in a small County Mayo pub, soon becomes the hero of the village when it is revealed that he has killed his tyrant of a father. Christy has the affections of a local widow—the publican's daughter, Pegeen Mike—and the other townspeople until old Mahan shows up wounded but very much alive. Despite these circumstances, Christy uses his new-found assurance to tame his father and then walks out on Pegeen Mike; he truly proves to be the "Playboy of the Western World."

In the opening of Act II, Christy, who now has "two fine women fighting for the likes of [him]," is cleaning a pair of Pegeen's boots and counting dinnerware in the pub.

◆ ◆ ◆ ◆

CHRISTY: (*To himself, counting jugs on dresser.*) Half a hundred beyond. Ten there. A score that's above. Eighty jugs. Six cups and a broken one. Two plates. A power of glasses. Bottles, a schoolmaster'd be hard set to count, and enough in them, I'm thinking, to drunken all the wealth and wisdom of the County Clare. (*He puts down the boot carefully.*) There's her boots now, nice and decent for her evening use, and isn't it grand brushes she has? (*He puts them down and goes by degrees to the looking glass.*) Well, this'd be a fine place to be my whole life talking out with swearing Christians, in place of my old dogs and cat, and I stalking around, smoking my pipe and drinking my fill, and never a day's work but drawing a cork an odd time, or wiping a glass, or rinsing out a shiny tumbler for a decent man. (*He takes the looking glass from the wall and puts it on the back of a chair; then sits down in front of it and begins washing his face.*) Didn't I know rightly I was handsome, though it was the divil's own mirror we had beyond, would twist a squint across an angel's brow; and I'll be growing fine from this day, the way I'll have a soft lovely skin on me and won't be the like of the clumsy young fellows do be ploughing all times in the earth and dung. (*He starts.*) Is she coming again? (*He looks out.*) Stranger girls. God help me, where'll I hide myself away and my long neck naked to the world? (*He looks out.*) I'd best go to the room maybe till I'm dressed again.

The Prison Cell

Mahmud Darwish; translated from the Arabic by Ben Bennani

A Young Man

The Prison Cell is a poem from Naomi Shihab Nye's anthology *This Same Sky, a Collection of Poems from Around the World.* Darwish's poem expresses the power of the human spirit – in this case a young Palestinian's – to escape the confinements that adversaries may impose.

YOUNG MAN: It is possible . . .
It is possible at least sometimes . . .
It is possible especially now
To ride a horse
Inside a prison cell
And run away . . .

It is possible for prison walls
To disappear,
For the cell to become a distant land
Without frontiers:

– What did you do with the walls?
– I gave them back to the rocks.
– And what did you do with the ceiling?
– I turned it into a saddle.
– And your chain?
– I turned it into a pencil.

The prison guard got angry.
He put an end to the dialogue.
He said he didn't care for poetry,
And bolted the door of my cell.

He came back to see me
In the morning;
He shouted at me:

– Where did all this water come from?
– I brought it from the Nile.
– And the trees?
– From the orchards of Damascus.
– And the music?
– From my heartbeat.

The prison guard got mad;
He put an end to my dialogue.
He said he didn't like my poetry,
And bolted the door of my cell.

But he returned in the evening:

– Where did this moon come from?
– From the nights of Baghdad.
– And the wine?
– From the vineyards of Algiers.
– And this freedom?
– From the chain you tied me with last night.

The prison guard grew so sad . . .
He begged me to give him back
His freedom.

A Raisin In The Sun
Lorraine Hansberry

Asagai, 18-20

Set in a Chicago ghetto in the 1950s, *A Raisin in the Sun* is the story of how three generations of the Younger family overcome their conflicts and bring their divergent hopes and dreams into common focus. After Walter Younger loses the family's savings, his sister Beneatha, who has had aspirations of becoming a physician, loses faith in the goodness of people and gives up her dream. However, in the speech that follows, Asagai, a student from Nigeria who has become friends with Beneatha, admonishes her not to give up hope or to believe that the truth about all people is that they are "puny, small and selfish."

ASAGAI: Truth? Why is it that you despairing ones always think that only you have the truth? I never thought to see *you* like that. You! Your brother made a stupid, childish mistake – and you are grateful to him. So that now you can give up the ailing human race on account of it. You talk about what good is struggle; what good is anything? Where are we all going? And why are we bothering?

[BENEATHA: *And you cannot answer it!* All your talk and dreams about Africa and Independence. Independence and then what? What about all the crooks and petty thieves and just plain idiots who will come into power to steal and plunder the same as before – only now they will be black and do it in the name of the new Independence – You cannot answer that.]

ASAGAI: [(*Shouting over her.*)] *I live the answer!* (*Pause.*) In my village at home it is the exceptional man who can even read a newspaper . . . or who ever *sees* a book at all. I will go home and much of what I will have to say will seem strange to the people of my village . . . But I will teach and work and things will happen, slowly and swiftly. At times it will seem that nothing changes at all . . . and then again . . . the sudden dramatic events which make history leap into the future. And then quiet again. Retrogression even. Guns, murder, revolution. And I even will have moments when I wonder if the quiet was not better than all that death and hatred. But I will look about my village at the illiteracy and disease

and ignorance and I will not wonder long. And perhaps . . .
perhaps I will be a great man . . . I mean perhaps I will hold on to
the substance of truth and find my way always with the right
course . . . and perhaps for it I will be butchered in my bed some
night by the servants of empire . . .

[BENEATHA: *The martyr!*]

ASAGAI: . . . or perhaps I shall live to be a very old man respected
and esteemed in my new nation . . . And perhaps I shall hold
office and this is what I'm trying to tell you, Alaiyo; perhaps the
things I believe now for my country will be wrong and outmoded,
and I will not understand and do terrible things to have things my
way or merely to keep my power. Don't you see that there will be
young men and women, not British soldiers then, but my own
black countrymen . . . to step out of the shadows some evening
and slit my then useless throat? Don't you see they have always
been there . . . that they always will be. And that such a thing as
my own death will be an advance? They who might kill me even
. . . actually replenish me!

Sideshow
Miguel Piñero

Clearnose Henry, 13-15

The characters in Miguel Piñero's *Sideshow* are Black and Puerto Rican teenagers – a collection of prostitutes, hustlers, drug dealers and pimps who present their lives in a series of improvised and real scenes. All have a unique story to share concerning their life on the streets and the danger and pain of existing on their own at such a young age. In the first speech, Clearnose Henry, a Puerto Rican glue-sniffer, introduces himself to the audience.

♦ ♦ ♦ ♦

CLEARNOSE HENRY: I'm Clearnose Henry. That's what everybody calls me. Clearnose Henry . . . 'cause I always clear my nose before I blow my mind. Costs me two first presidents to buy me a box of tubes and coin Lincolns to cop my dream brown paper bag. I don't slink around corners under street lamps to score, or hide in some dim lighted muggers' tenement hall for my pusher to appear. That bag is for dope fiends and that scene is a dragpot. Grass is too scarce in these parts and I'm scared of scag 'cause I'm scared of needles . . . faint at the sight of one. That's why I don't watch those doctor shows on TV. Excuse me a second while I pour my tubes into my dream brown paper bag. Yeah man, that looks pretty good. Like I was saying, snuff is for old people who like to sit and nod and LSD or sunshine . . . those trips they take you on are too far out . . . speed kills . . . oh, oh, . . . the sleep sand is raining out the bottom of my dream brown paper bag. I'm going to do it, ain't gonna talk it.

♦ ♦ ♦ ♦

In Clearnose's second speech, we see elements of the young man's source of pain and the reason for his drug addiction; he is alone on the roof.

CLEARNOSE: The city is drowning under tons of tubes of glue. Wow, the sky has backed away and the stars are doing the bugaloo blues. The buildings look like giant tubes of glue and the garbage cans hold mountains of jewels sparkling for my eyes to see. Man, I is a prophet. I am Jesus Christ reincarnated, one of the most outasight images I've pulled from my dream brown paper bag. Can you imagine a world without glue? You gots to have glue, you need it to hold the world together. . . and it's store bought. I better keep my imagination open for the cops. They found out I was with Frankie. He was my gluehead partner. We used to paste the world together up on the roofs, in the school toilets, in the subway trains. Oh, yeah, I was with him when he jumped into the tracks. That's the day the A-train became the B, dig it, B for blood. Wow, don't you git it? It's a heavy joke. I mean, like the dude was all over the place: head one way, arms another, leg on the platform, a very un-together person. Man, like it ain't like I pushed him into the tracks. Like I don't know what they want me for . . . you know like . . . you know what I mean, you know? Right, take me a short visit into my dream brown paper bag. Yeah, that's cool. Losing much of its power now. Oh, I wish everybody would stop saying how much they care and love.

♦ ♦ ♦ ♦

Malo, 15-16
In this final speech, Malo, the "Merchant," explains his trade to the audience.

MALO: Thirty-five dollars for a Bulogine . . . some people you can see them coming a mile away . . .a seven dollar Timex with a famous label. Hi, I'm Malo the Merchant. Malo in Spanish means bad, not bad as in bad, but bad as in good. They call me Malo the Merchant because I'm good at what I do. I'm so good, it's terrible. It's bad, that's why I'm Malo-bad. Can you dig it? What do I do? You just witnessed me in action. Some of my friends say I can talk the handle off a pot. I've never tried, but I don't doubt that I can do it. That's one of the tools of my trade: my tongue and these labels. I got all kinds of labels. The little woman at home hard at work sewing on famous labels on second-hand clothes. After I take them out the cleaners, just like new. Maybe you'll like a suit . . . very cheap . . . (*Laughs.*) . . . yeah . . . I can take a cheaply made TV set from some obscure company from a country you never even heard of and give glory with my labels and with my tongue . . . here, take a look at this tongue of mine . . . see it . . . all red with the fire of speech. I could have been a preacher . . . hell-fire and brimstone . . . don't think I ain't hip to the mind game . . . turned around collar . . . shit, only thing is my words kept falling out of the bible . . . and then once I got caught in bed with the preacher's wife . . . weren't too bad . . . if he hadn't decided to join us . . . three is a crowd. Malo the Merchant . . . I like my own name . . . it's got a certain ring to it . . . everybody needs some type of recognition . . . I ain't no different than anyone else. I thought of being a dealer one time, but like you really don't make no bread. If you is a small timer, too many people to be paid, too many people come up short. Burglary is climbing too high and as you go up, so can you come down. I hate mugging. First of all, you're taking someone's payday check, 'cause not many mug the big execs. As a merchant I only take what they were goin' to waste on beers in some greasy spoon saloon. Then sometime you hit a drunk that wants to fight and you got to off him or he vomits all over you and you stink so bad ain't no pusher wanna sell you a thing. Now, I know, 'cause you see me greasy as a porkchop you think I stink. Well, this is only an accessory of my trade. I got more veins at home than a little bit . . . got it like the feds . . . everyone likes to deal and wheel. Me, I just wheel the deals. I got something for everybody. Nobody goes away empty-handed when you come and see Malo the Merchant. . . . White boys from the suburbs . . . in a way I am the cause of the state's great concern with drugs nowadays. When they came to me, I got it for them . . . never turn one of them down. They came, I have, they took and they all got hooked, kinda like a poem. That's when dope became a terrible plague, destroying the youth of your nation. Well, not my nation, their nation, 'cause for years it had been destroying our nation and no one gave a good fuck about it. Hey, what you wanna git, whitey? Hey, whacha wanna git, Mr. Jones? You wanna nicey girlie to fuckie fuckie? I got two of everything, three of anything and you got to start out with one of nothing so you can end up with something. Someone at sometime has been taken for his poke by the sleight of hand of the Murphy Man or the words some con man spoke. Now, the dope fiends are ruining the name of a hell of a game. When are we gonna yell out no more fucking dope? You are surprised that I, a dope fiend, would make such a distinction between me and my peers? But you see, the time before this there was the time before that and that's where I live, in the time before this.

The Slab Boys
John Byrne

Phil, 19

"The Slab Boys" of John Byrne's title are three young men who work mixing and matching paints for a carpet company in Scotland. Each of the boys dreams of a better life, perhaps a future that would elevate their place in the world beyond that of their parents. Phil dreams of going to art school but is constantly worried that the mental illness that has tormented his mother for years is somehow in his future as well. In the first speech, Phil tells Spanky (a fellow slab boy) about a time his mother took him to visit a convalescent home. It was sometime after this visit that Phil's mother started being hospitalized from time to time as a result of her mental illness.

◆ ◆ ◆ ◆

PHIL: Did I ever tell you about that convalescent home my Maw and me went to? At the seaside . . . West Kilbride . . .

[SPANKY: Don't think so.]

PHIL: I was about eleven at the time. Got took out of school to go with her . . . on the train. Some holiday. Place was choc-a-bloc with invalids . . . headcases soaking up the Clyde breeze before getting pitched back into the hurly-burly of everyday life . . . Old-age pensioners, their skulls full of mush . . . single guys in their forties in too-short trousers and intellects to match . . . Middle-aged women in ankle socks roaming about looking for a letter box to stick their postcards through. Abject bloody misery, it was. Dark-brown waxcloth you could see your face in . . . bathroom mirrors you couldn't. Lights out at half seven . . . no wireless, no comics, no nothing. Compulsory hymn-singing for everybody including the bed-ridden. Towels that tore the skin off your bum when you had a bath. Steamed fish on Sundays for a special treat . . .

[SPANKY: Bleagh . . .]

PHIL: The one highlight was a doll of about nineteen or twenty . . . There we all were sitting in our deck chairs in the sun-lounge . . . curtains drawn . . . listening for the starch wearing out on the Matron's top lip . . . when this doll appears at the door, takes a couple of hops into the room, then turns this cartwheel right down the middle of the two rows of deckchairs . . . lands on her pins . . . daraaaaa! Brilliant! I started to laugh and got a skelp on the nut. The Matron was beeling . . .

[SPANKY: About the skelp?]

PHIL: [About the doll's cartwheel, stupid.] Two old dears had to get carried up to their rooms with palpitations and a guy with a lavvy brush moustache wet himself. It was the high spot of the holiday.

◆ ◆ ◆ ◆

In this speech, Phil has just been told that his mother has escaped the mental hospital. In his fright and anger he attacks Alan.

PHIL: [I bet you he doesn't.] (*To Alan.*) What do you know about getting up in the middle of the night in your shirt tail to say five decades of the rosary over your Maw's open wrists? What do you know about screaming fits and your old man's nut getting bopped off the Pope's calendar? What do you know about razor blades and public wards and row upon row of gumsy cadavers all sitting up watching you stumble in with your Lucozade and excuses? Christ, what one's mine? Is that you, Maw? What do you know about living in a rabbit hutch with concrete floors and your Old Man's never in and you're left trying to have a conversation with a TV set and a Maw that thinks you're St. Thomas Aquinas? What do you know about standing there day in, day out in the Factor's office asking for a move and the guy with the shiny arse on his trousers shakes his head and treats your Old Dear like dirt??

Solado Razo

Luis Valdez

Johnny, 18-20

Luis Valdez wrote *Soldado Razo* in 1971, in part, for the Chicano Moratorium on the War in Vietnam. The short play revolves around the story of Johnny, a young Chicano soldier killed in Vietnam. In the first speech, Johnny reflects on the life he is about to leave behind as he goes to war.

♦ ♦ ♦ ♦

JOHNNY: Chihuahua, pobre jefita. Mañana va a ser muy duro para ella. También para mí. It was pretty hard when I went to boot camp, ¿pero ahora? Vietnam! 'Ta cabrón, man. The jefito también. I'm not going to be here to help him out. No me estaba haciendo rico en el jale, but it was something. Una alivianada siquiera. El carnalillo no puede trabajar todavía porque está en la escuela. I hope he stays there también. And finishes. A mí nunca me cayó ese jale, but I know the carnalillo digs it. He's smart too. Maybe he'll even go to college. One of us has got to make it in this life. Me, I guess I'll just get married con Cecilia and have a bola de chavalos. I remember when I first saw her at the Rainbow. I couldn't even dance with her porque me había echado mis birrias. The next week was pretty good, though. Desde entonces. How long ago was that? June . . . no, July. Four months. Ahora me quiero ranar con ella. Her parents don't like me, I know. They think I'm a vago. Maybe they'll feel different when I come back from Nam. Simón, el war veteran! Maybe I'll get wounded and come back con un chingatal de medals. I wonder how the vatos around here are going to think about that? Pinche barrio. I've lived here all my life. Now I'm going to Vietnam. I might even get killed. If I do, they'll bring me back here in a box, covered with the flag . . . military funeral like they gave Pete Gómez . . . everybody crying . . . la jefita. What am I thinking, man? ¡Estoy loco!

♦ ♦ ♦ ♦

The second speech is a letter home.

JOHNNY: 'Amá, there's a lot happening here that I didn't know about before. I don't know if I'm allowed to write about it, pero voy a hacer la lucha. Yesterday we attacked a small village near some rice paddies. We had orders to kill everybody because they were supposed to be V-Cs, comunistas. We entered the small pueblito and my buddies comenzaron a disparar. I saw one of them kill an old man and an old lady. My sergeant killed a small boy about seven years old, then he shot his mother or some woman that came running up crying. Blood was everywhere. I don't remember what happened after that, but my sergeant ordered me to start shooting. I think I did. May God forgive me for what I did, but I never wanted to come over here. They say we have to do it to defend our country.

[MAMA: Hijo, me da tristeza con lo que nos escribes. Hablé con tu padre y también se puso muy triste, pero dice que así es la guerra. Tu recuerda que estás peleando con comunistas. Tengo una vela prendida allá por donde andas y que te regrese a nuestros brazos bueno y sano.]

JOHNNY: 'Amá, I had a dream la otra noche. I dreamed I was breaking into one of the hooches, así le decimos a las casas de los vietnameses. I went in firing my M-16 porque sabía que el village estabe controlado por los gooks. I killed three of them right away, but when I looked down it was mi 'Apá, el carnalillo and you, jefita. I don't know how much more I can stand. Please tell Sapo and all the vatos how it's like over here. Don't let them . . .

The Sound Of Waves
Yukio Mishima; translated by Meredith Watherby

Shinji, 18-20

Yukio Mishima was one of the leading Japanese writers of fiction and drama in the 20th Century. *The Sound of Waves* is a short novel recounting the first love of a boy and girl growing up in a small Japanese fishing village. Although this story is simply told, the struggle of Shinji to win the love of the beautiful Hatsue is a compelling, universal picture of young love the world over. In a village where work is everything, Shinji and Hatsue steal brief, important moments together that build their love for one another. In the speech below, Shinji, in a precious few hours alone with Hatsue, shares his dreams of a future that is both plentiful and peaceful.

◆ ◆ ◆ ◆

SHINJI: As for me, some day I want to buy a coastal freighter with the money I've worked for and saved, and then go into the shipping business with my brother, carrying lumber from Kishu and coal from Kyushu . . . Then I'll have my mother take it easy, and when I get old I'll come back to the island and take it easy too. . . . No matter where I sail, I'll never forget our island. . . . It has the most beautiful scenery in all Japan – every person on Uta-jima was firmly convinced of this – and in the same way I'll do my best to help make life on our island the most peaceful there is anywhere . . . the happiest there is anywhere . . . Because if we don't do that, everybody will start forgetting the island and quit wanting to come back. No matter how much times change, very bad things – very bad ways – will all always disappear before they get to our island. . . . The sea – it only brings the good and right things that the island needs . . . and keeps the good and right things we already have here. . . . That's why there's not a thief on the whole island – nothing but brave, manly people – people who always have the will to work truly and well and put up with whatever comes – people whose love is never double-faced – people with nothing mean about them anywhere . . .

Take A Giant Step
Louis Peterson

Spence, early teens

Take a Giant Step depicts the coming of age of Spence, a young African-American boy who experiences a sense of estrangement from his white friends as he emerges into adulthood. Confused by the prejudices of the adult world, his anger leads to his expulsion from school and a series of low-life encounters that leave him even more bewildered. It is not until he has a confrontation with his parents, confides his fears to the family maid, and experiences the death of his grandmother that he is able to make sense of what he may become. In the speech that follows, Spence tells his grandmother why he got kicked out of school.

♦ ♦ ♦ ♦

SPENCE: Today [in history class] we started talking about the Civil War and one of the smart little skirts at the back of the room wanted to know why the Negroes in the South didn't rebel against slavery. Why did they wait for the Northerners to come down and help them? And this Miss Crowley went on to explain how they were stupid and didn't have sense enough to help themselves. Well, anyway, Gram, when she got through talking they sounded like the worst morons that ever lived and I began to wonder how they'd managed to live a few thousand years all by themselves in Africa with nobody's help. I would have let it pass – see – except that the whole class was whispering and giggling and turning around and looking at me – so I got up and just stood next to my desk looking at her. She looked at me for a couple of minutes and asked me if perhaps I had something to say in the discussion. I said I might have a lot of things to say if I didn't have to say them in the company of such dumb jerks. Then I asked her frankly what college she went to.

[GRANDMA: What did she say?]

SPENCE: She told me I was being impudent. I told her it was not my intention to be impudent but I would honestly like to know. So she puts one hand on her hip – kinda throwing the other hip out of joint at the same time – and like she wants to spit on me she says "Scoville." Then I says, "And they didn't teach you nothing about the *up*rising of the slaves during the Civil War – or Frederick Douglass?" She says, "No – they didn't." "In that case," I said, "I don't want to be in your crummy history class." And I walk out of the room. When I get out in the hall, Gram, I'm shaking, I'm so mad – and I had this cigar I was going to sell for a sundae. I knew I couldn't eat a sundae now 'cause it would just make me sick so – I just had to do something so I went into the Men's Room and smoked the cigar. I just had about two drags on the thing when in comes the janitor and hauls me down to old Hasbrook's office – and when I get down there – there's Miss Crowley and old Hasbrook talking me over in low tones – and in five short minutes he'd thrown me out of school.

Welcome Home Jacko
Mustapha Matura

Zippy, 17-21

Mustapha Matura, perhaps the leading dramatist of West Indian origin, wrote *Welcome Home Jacko* after visiting a community youth center in Sheffield, England. The center was a place for young people to socialize apart from the pangs of social oppression and racism. The play, set in just such a center, concerns a group of young people struggling for a Black identity. As the four young West Indians interact in the club, exploring their place in the world, they assert their beliefs. Sandy, the white girl who manages the club, is preparing to welcome home Jacko, who has spent the last five years in prison for raping a girl. In the first speech Zippy, in Rastafarian robe, explains to Jacko why he and his friends like gathering at the center.

♦ ♦ ♦ ♦

ZIPPY: Cha yes is a good place man. Dis is de only place in dis town whey we could come an relax an en get no harassment. We could do we own ting here, an dey en have nobody ter tell we what ter do or asking we what we doing. If we go by de corner, is Panda Car come up, ter ask we question, Ras clart, dem do' like ter see we doing notting. Everybody must be doing someting, working or going somewhere or coming from somewhere. If dem see people relaxing dem tink dem up ter someting. Dem people do' relax so dem do' like ter see people relax. Dem like ter have heart attack an give people dem heart attack.

♦ ♦ ♦ ♦

Jacko, 20-25

In the second speech Jacko tells Sandy why the Rastafarian dreams and hopes expressed by the young men in the center are nothing to him but unrealistic nonsense.

JACKO: All dat is foolishness too. Ethiopia is a Marxist country an Haile Selassie is dead an he exploit he own people more dan anybody. Dat en true blackness, blackness is seeing tings de way it is nothing more. Inside, inside prison. I was in prison, but me en know whey all yer was. I read all de time I in dey, everyting, I read about how de National Front an dem terrorising black people an nobody en doing notting, an how dis Rastaman ting saying peace and love an smoking dope an dreaming bout Africa an de Bible, and de National Front attacking people. I car understand all yer. Wha happen, all yer car see, all yer blind? I say wen I come out I go meet de youth fighting back, because de paper en go print dem ting, an I go join dem. But de paper right. Wen I went in people eye was opening, now I come out it close. Wha happen, wha happen ter all yer? We fight de racist in prison. All yer outside, wha all yer do?

The Young Graduates
Victor Rozov; translated by Miriam Morton

Andrei, 17

Set in former Soviet Russia, *The Young Graduates* defends the right of its young
characters to assert their individuality and to make their own decisions
concerning the course of their lives. Rozov defends young people's rights to
criticize the shortcomings of society, including adults and parents who behave in
hypocritical ways. Likewise, the play reinforces the values that make the
individual and society spiritually strong and dynamic. In the speech below,
Andrei, a young man who recently graduated from a Moscow 10-year school (an
accelerated program) has been attempting to prepare for his college entrance
exams and to find his "calling" in life.

◆ ◆ ◆ ◆

ANDREI: I come to the school. There's a mob of "aspirants" – as
usual. Everyone's eyes are bleary from cramming and tense with
worry. And me? I couldn't care less. Next I see a pitiful looking girl
standing in a corner. Too thin, with wispy blond hair in little braids
the width of my finger. Dressed so-so, no frills whatever. She
stands there, pale and frightened hugging her books and
mumbling something to herself – maybe still memorizing
something, or praying . . . I couldn't tell. I tell you, the sight of her
depressed me, and I thought to myself, what business have I to be
here – maybe I'd do her out of a place. I don't give a damn – but it
means everything to her . . . and to so many others, too. So I
turned around and left. That was dumb, wasn't it?

[ALEKSEI: What do you plan to do instead?]

[ANDREI: There you go – you, too – asking the same idiotic
question! You see, I don't know, but this is what I believe –
eveyone has his particular aptitude.]

[ALEKSEI: So?]

ANDREI: Well, I mean his proper niche – the only thing that's right
for him. You find it, and all your energies well up to the surface.
You give it all you've got. You are satisfied with life, others like
you and value you. It's most important to find that special niche.
Take you – you feel where yours is, and so do others. But me – I
have no idea. None. But it's somewhere. I want to find it. A
desired vocation, a calling is probably a magnet to that niche.
What do you think?